ROUTLEDGE LIBRARY EDITIONS BROADCASTING

Volume 15

BROADCASTING IN MEXICO

BROADCASTING IN MEXICO

LUIS ANTONIO DE NORIEGA
AND
FRANCES LEACH

LONDON AND NEW YORK

First published in 1979 by Routledge & Kegan Paul Ltd

This edition first published in 2024
by Routledge
4 Park Square, Milton Park, Abingdon, Oxon OX14 4RN

and by Routledge
605 Third Avenue, New York, NY 10158

Routledge is an imprint of the Taylor & Francis Group, an informa business

© 1979 International Institute of Communications

All rights reserved. No part of this book may be reprinted or reproduced or utilised in any form or by any electronic, mechanical, or other means, now known or hereafter invented, including photocopying and recording, or in any information storage or retrieval system, without permission in writing from the publishers.

Trademark notice: Product or corporate names may be trademarks or registered trademarks, and are used only for identification and explanation without intent to infringe.

British Library Cataloguing in Publication Data
A catalogue record for this book is available from the British Library

ISBN: 978-1-032-59391-3 (Set)
ISBN: 978-1-032-60768-9 (Volume 15) (hbk)
ISBN: 978-1-032-60769-6 (Volume 15) (pbk)
ISBN: 978-1-003-46046-6 (Volume 15) (ebk)

DOI: 10.4324/9781003460466

Publisher's Note
The publisher has gone to great lengths to ensure the quality of this reprint but points out that some imperfections in the original copies may be apparent.

Disclaimer
The publisher has made every effort to trace copyright holders and would welcome correspondence from those they have been unable to trace.

BROADCASTING IN MEXICO

Luis Antonio de Noriega
and Frances Leach

CASE STUDIES ON BROADCASTING SYSTEMS

ROUTLEDGE & KEGAN PAUL
London, Henley and Boston
in association with
INTERNATIONAL INSTITUTE OF COMMUNICATIONS

First published in 1979
by Routledge & Kegan Paul Ltd
39 Store Street,
London WC1E 7DD,
Broadway House,
Newtown Road,
Henley-on-Thames,
Oxon RG9 1EN and
9 Park Street,
Boston, Mass. 02108, USA
Printed in Great Britain by
Redwood Burn Ltd
Trowbridge and Esher
© International Institute of Communications 1979
No part of this book may be reproduced in
any form without permission from the
publisher, except for the quotation of brief
passages in criticism.

ISBN   0 7100 04168

CONTENTS

FOREWORD by Asa Briggs		vii
ACKNOWLEDGMENTS		xi
INTRODUCTION		xiii

1 NATIONAL ENVIRONMENT FOR BROADCASTING — 1
  1 Geography — 1
  2 Language — 2
  3 Population — 2
  4 Cultural heritage — 4
  5 Government and politics — 6
  6 Economy — 8
  7 Education — 11
  8 Telecommunications — 11
  9 Mass media — 13

2 THE ADVENT AND DEVELOPMENT OF BROADCASTING IN MEXICO — 15
  1 Radio: the beginnings (1921-9) — 15
  2 Television: the beginnings (1950-60) — 20

3 BROADCASTING STRUCTURES AND REGULATORY FRAMES — 27
  1 Antecedents of the 1960 Federal Law of Radio and Television — 27
  2 1960 Federal Law of Radio and Television — 29

4 COMMERCIAL AND NON-COMMERCIAL RADIO — 37
  1 Commercial radio — 37
  2 Cultural and educational radio — 43
  3 Additional radio and audio-visual educational campaigns — 48

5	COMMERCIAL AND NON-COMMERCIAL TELEVISION	49
	1 Technical development	51
	2 Televisa	53
	3 Channel 13: the Corporación Mexicana de Radio y Televisión	64
	4 Non-commercial and cultural television	69
6	THE FUTURE OF MEXICAN BROADCASTING	75
	APPENDICES	82
	1 Map of Mexico	82
	2 Map of Televisa's TV networks	83
	3 Televisa: comparative analysis of broadcasting hours and local foreign production, per year (June 1976-7)	84
	4 Direccion General de Radio, Television y Cinematografia: organisation chart	85
	5 Televisa: organisation chart	86
	BIBLIOGRAPHY	87

FOREWORD

In many different parts of the world official and unofficial enquiries, often protracted, are being carried out concerning the future of broadcasting. Some of them have recently been completed. In every case two points have almost immediately become clear. First, the future of broadcasting can never be completely separated from its past, even though the history of broadcasting in all countries is a recent one: there may be sharp breaks, not all of which are registered in legislation, but there are also continuities. Second, the future, like the past, will not depend on technological development alone. There are many exciting new communications technologies, many of them still in their early stages, but the speed and scope of their development will be determined by social, economic, political and cultural factors as well as by the technologies themselves. It has always been so.

Common technologies have been employed in different ways in different countries - sometimes with a few measures of control imposed by governments, by professional groups, or by trade unions, often with many. It is remarkable to what a great extent it is necessary to understand the general history of particular countries in order to understand what they have done with their conscious or unconscious communications policies.

This series of monographs, sponsored by the International Institute of Communications, is intended to direct attention to the main features of the communications patterns of a number of different countries. The studies deal with broadcasting structures rather than with the detailed processes of programme making or with the diffusion of news and ideas; and they seek first to explain how these structures came into existence, second, to identify what have been the landmarks in their histories, and, third, to elucidate what are the alternative possibilities envisaged for the future. Of course, a knowledge of the structures by itself is not enough to enable an adequate evaluation to be made of the quality of broadcasting output in any particular case. The same structure will generate different output at different times, and very similar structures will generate very different outputs.

Until recently it was thought possible to distinguish broadly between on the one hand systems controlled by government and on the other hand systems linked with business through private enterprise and advertising. Yet there was always a third type of system, represented formidably by the BBC, which entailed neither government control nor business underpinning. This system, which was widely copied, was seldom copied in its entirety, and it now has many variants, most of which have deviated substantially from the model. In many countries there are now dual or multiple systems, in some cases, but not in all, subject to common 'supervision'; and in all countries there are degrees and nuances of control of broadcasting output whether by governments or by market forces.

The United States system, which is important not only in itself but because of the influence it has through exports of programmes and through diffusion of broadcasting styles, is itself a complex system - containing as it does a multiplicity of agencies and a changing public service element. It is hoped that United States experience will be covered in a later volume. There is increasing pressure there for a major review in the light of that experience and of continuing technological change affecting not only broadcasting but a wide and increasingly interrelated group of new communications technologies.

Alongside complex national structures, the products of time and place and in many cases deeply resistant to fundamental change, there are, of course, many new broadcasting structures in the world, including many which have come into existence in recent years in new countries. Many of these structures reveal themselves as extremely complex, too, when they are subjected to careful scrutiny. Nor are they necessarily very malleable. The more governments set out to chart and carry through conscious 'communications policies' - often related directly to their planning policies - the more they are compelled to consider the relationship of 'traditional' modes of communication to new technologies. The more, too, they are forced to establish priorities. This series includes, therefore, a number of countries where such policies have been formulated or are in the course of formulation.

Measuring the distance between policy formulation and policy implementation or effectiveness is, of course, at least as difficult in this field as in any other, and interesting work is being carried out by scholars in several countries on promise and performance. This series of studies, however, is less ambitious in intention. The studies are designed to provide accessible and reliable information rather than to evaluate the quality of achievement. The first cases chosen include some where there is no existing manageable monograph and some where the particular experience of that country is of general interest at the present time. The countries selected include some which are old and some which are new, some which are big and some which are small.

As the series unfolds, there will be increasing scope for comparison and contrast, and international patterns will doubtless be revealed - of 'models', of 'imports' and 'exports', of regional 'exchanges', and of relationships between different media. As such comparison and contrast become more sophisticated than they have been in the past, any conclusions reached will be of increasing value in the future to those policy makers who are concerned to see their own circumstances in perspective and to frame their choices clearly.

Meanwhile, the International Institute of Communications, formerly called the International Broadcast Institute, which first launched this series, will continue to concern itself with the general opportunities and problems associated with the continuing advance of communications technology. The Institute is an international body which seeks to bring together engineers and social scientists, lawyers and programme-makers, academics and administrators.

The author of each case study in this series has been free to assemble and to present material relating to his own country in a manner decided upon by him, and he alone is responsible for the evidence offered and for the conclusions reached. Yet guidelines have been given him about arrangement and coverage. Thus, he has been encouraged to ask questions as well as to compile facts. What have been the critical points in the history of broadcasting? How have that history and the broadcasting structures which have been evolved been related to the history of other forms of communication (the Press, for example)? What are the main institutional relationships at the present time? What are likely to be the future trends? Is it possible to talk of an integrated 'communications policy' in the case of the country under review?

The International Institute of Communications has no views of its own as an institution on the answers to such questions, but its Trustees and members believe that answers should be forthcoming if debate is to be both lively and well informed. Much of the serious study of communications systems has hitherto been carried out within the confines, cultural as well as political, of national boundaries, and it is such research which most easily secures financial support. This series will point in a different direction. It is not only comparison and contrast which are necessary but a grasp of what problems and opportunities are common to countries, not necessarily alone but in the great continental broadcasting unions or other groupings between states.

We can now trace the beginnings of a 'global' sense in communications studies. Indeed, the word 'beginning' may be misleading. The sense certainly long preceded the use of satellites and was anticipated in much of the nineteenth century literature. The world was being pulled together; it was becoming a smaller place; everyone, everywhere, it was suggested, would be drawn in, instantaneously.

Communications policies, of course, have often failed to unite: instead, they have pulled people apart in clashes of images as well as in wars of words. And some of the case studies in this series will show how.

Two final points should be made. First, nothing stands still in communications history, and there are bound to be changes between the writing of these case studies and their publication. The processes of implementation of policy changes are often protracted. Second, it may well be that we are moving out of the age of 'mass broadcasting' as we have understood it into a new age of electronic communication. In that case, these studies will appear at a strategic time and will deserve careful study separately and together.

Asa Briggs
Worcester College, Oxford

ACKNOWLEDGMENTS

First and foremost, sincere thanks are due to Miguel Alemán Velasco, a prominent figure in the Mexican broadcasting industry, who made this case study possible. Gratitude is also due to Raúl Lomelí for his invaluable assistance and guidance as coordinator, and to Juan José Miró whose great encouragement and factual input was vital to the study. Finally, a very special thank you is due to Myron Gold, who was always there to provide immeasurable help in correcting the manuscript and to feed us with ideas and points of view which certainly enriched our work.

LAN
FL

The International Institute of Communications is most grateful to the Fundacion Cultural Televisa, A.C., for its assistance in financing this study on Mexican broadcasting, and to the Hoso-Bunka Foundation, Inc., for its assistance in financing the series of case studies on broadcasting systems.

INTRODUCTION

This study traces the birth and growth of Mexico's broadcasting services against the background of her country's geographical, cultural, demographic, economic and political structure. The background sketch is provided because only with some indication of 'the Mexican reality' can the essential character of the country's radio and television industry be understood.

The development of Mexican radio and television has been characterised by innovation and experiment by both government and private enterprise. Sometimes the country has been the beneficiary of these efforts and sometimes it has been the victim. Establishing mass communications in Mexico with their necessarily vast economic and technical infrastructure has not been an easy task. Up to a certain point, the cultural infrastructure of the country itself dictated the path taken by the media. But there have been temptations to imitate the established structures of other countries. It has always been necessary to combat these temptations and to ensure a reasonable freedom from foreign interference and influence and also a programme content reflecting the country's needs and progress.

Faced with urgent choices and forced to make rapid decisions, Mexico's media evolved into the idiosyncratic institutions, with their unique forms, that we know today. This study tries to present the struggles, the problems and the solutions involved in these exciting and rewarding attempts to create an authentically autonomous communications industry. We hope that the portrayal of these concepts may serve to illuminate and help explain similar situations as they occur in the birth and the expansion of communications industries all over the world.

Miguel Alemán Velasco
Mexico City

INTRODUCTION

Chapter 1

NATIONAL ENVIRONMENT FOR BROADCASTING

It is never easy to capture in a few words the feeling of the environment in which a national broadcasting system evolves. However, there is one impression and one word which emerges in all descriptions, by nationals and foreigners alike, of Mexico: drama. Its geography, history, art and architecture, whether ancient or modern, seem imbued with a sense of the dramatic, of high colour, hidden contrasts. It is difficult to keep alive this sense of drama in what after all should be a factual account but it is this dramatic quality that provides the background to all that follows.

1 GEOGRAPHY

The United States of Mexico covers an area of 1,972,546 sq. kms, making it the fourteenth largest country in the world and the third largest in Latin America. It has common borders with the United States of America to the north and Guatemala and Belize to the south. The proximity of the United States, which borders Mexico for approximately 3,115 kms, has greatly influenced the historical, political and economic development of the country.

The influence of the North has been a constant element in the country's history, since even the original inhabitants were part of the waves of population movements which in prehistoric times swept southward across the continent. During the 'colonial era' (1519-1821) Mexico's geographical situation made it an ideal link for trade between the Far East and the West. By the end of the nineteenth and in the early twentieth century, it was thought that Mexico would be the perfect location for a canal between the Pacific and the Atlantic Oceans. The construction was to be across the Isthmus of Tehuantepec, but this project was abandoned in favour of what is now the Panama Canal.

Mexico consists mainly of a broad, central plateau, flanked on both sides by mountain ranges which separate the plateau from the hot central lowlands. In such a mountainous country the difficulty of getting from place to place has hindered progress and has affected the expansion and growth of the broadcasting system.

The southern half of Mexico lies within the tropics but the altitude in most areas keeps the climate fairly cool, except in the deserts of the north. Basically, the country may be divided by climate into three zones: *tierra fria* (cold), *tierra templada* (temperate) and *tierra caliente* (hot). The cold zone is associated with the mountainous regions (above 1,830 metres) where oak trees grow and, on the higher slopes, fir and pines. Wheat, maize and beans are cultivated. The temperate zone is lower, and tobacco and tomatoes are grown. Below lie the hot lands, the rainy regions, with tropical trees and crops such as cotton, cocoa, rice, rubber and sugar.

2 LANGUAGE

Spanish is the official language and is spoken by 97.9 per cent of the population. According to the 1970 census, 7.8 per cent speak an indigenous tongue in addition to Spanish. About one million people (2.1 per cent) speak only their indigenous tongue.

Apart from the difficulty in communicating with these indigenous speakers, there are no barriers to understanding among the different regions of the country, in spite of the different accents and regional dialects. The Mexico City accent is the most influential and since the main television and radio production centres are in the capital it is commonly used in radio and television programmes.

3 POPULATION

Mexico's population has increased considerably in the last thirty years from just over 19.5 million in 1940 to almost 35 million in 1960. It reached nearly 62 million in 1976.

Chapter 1

The population explosion is due to a high birth rate and a sharp drop in the mortality rate – now one of the lowest in the world at 8.6 per thousand. This reflects in general the improved quality of the economic and social services and relates specifically to advances in preventive medicine. The annual growth rate is currently one of the highest in the world. It is estimated that Mexico's population will be about 71 million in 1980.

The ethnic composition of the population is 55 per cent *mestizo* (a mixture of the indigenous people and the Spanish colonisers), 29 per cent Indian, 15 per cent European and 1 per cent of other races. Two-thirds of the European population are native born. The rest are immigrants – mainly from Spain, the United States and France.

The population is unevenly distributed. In 1976, 58 per cent was concentrated centrally in eleven of the country's thirty-two states. Here the population density is over 100 inhabitants per square kilometre, while other large areas in the north and southwest have fewer than 10. Mexico City alone, in 1976, contained 20.26 per cent of the entire population, with a density of 4,585 inhabitants per sq. km.

Immigration has been relatively unimportant in recent years, the last notable migratory movement being that of Spanish refugees at the end of the Spanish Civil War. On the other hand, many Mexicans, especially farm workers, have emigrated to the United States in search of employment and higher wages.

Large-scale migration from rural to urban areas, especially to central Mexico, has caused a wide range of urban problems including both unemployment and underemployment, shortages of social services and the accelerated creation of suburban slums. In 1970, the urban population stood at 59 per cent as compared with 49 per cent in 1960. A serious consequence of the mass exodus to the cities has been the decline of agricultural production.

Because of the high birth rate and the constantly declining rate of infant mortality, nearly 59 per cent of the population is under twenty years old, with 26 per cent under forty and 18 per cent over forty.

4 CULTURAL HERITAGE

In its origins Mexico was Indian and Spanish; now it has its own personality. The strength of this personality depends not only on the Spanish past but also on the Indian past. This basic evaluation reappears in various forms in all writings about Mexico, and particularly in the Mexican's preoccupation with his past.

Mexico has a long history, much longer than the Spanish *conquistadores* expected when they first landed on the eastern coast in 1519. Through the efforts of the archaeologists, the account of this history has been constantly pushed back to that period some 30,000 years ago when the first inhabitants of the Americas crossed Bering's Straits and spread over the continent.

The early Meso-american cultures seem to have grown and developed in relative isolation from the rest of the world. The first high cultures already present those distinct features which in varying degrees characterise all that follow. With the Olmec culture (2000/1500-600 BC), certain basic themes are already discernible which are developed by the following cultures: the Maya, the Tollec, the Huastec, the Mixtec, the Zapotec, the Totonec, and finally the Aztecs, newcomers on a stage that had witnessed the rise and fall of many civilisations.

As in any group of cultures, there are many themes and many variations on those themes, but some appear as more typical and specific than others. An inventory of crops shows what the rest of the world owed to these cultures: at various points in the sequence maize, beans, squash, avocado, chile, pumpkin, tobacco, cocoa and other significant plants were domesticated. An obsession with the seasons and with time resulted in astronomic observations far beyond those available in Europe at the same period. Measurements of the solar year - so precise that they have only been surpassed with the use of modern instruments - included the discovery of the lunar month and the revolutions of Venus and other planets, all combined in an intricate, interlocking series of calendars which regulated ritual and social life. In the same vein, the Mesoamerican cultures invented writing, positional mathematics based on a vigesimal system, and the zero. Particularly distinctive of the Classic period (300-900 AD) is the emergence of massive architectural centres with pyramid temples, plazas, dormitories, shrines, ballcourts, adoratorios ornamented with shrine sculpture, painting, stucco and clay modelling. Social systems evolved from tribal societies, via a chiefdom stage to city states and urban civilisation and finally to an 'imperialistic' stage of which the embryonic 'empire' of the Aztecs is the final example.

In the Meso-american cultures, nature, science and religion were interwoven in patterns reflected in art and architecture, in mythology, ritual and belief. Even today, remnants of those attitudes towards divinity, authority and magic still survive.

Among the poorly educated it is common to turn to *curanderos* (healers) and *bruja* (witches) for solutions to daily problems. A more orthodox religious fervour has been a recurrent strand in Mexican life. In modern times, many have turned to the secular figures of authority in government who are often regarded with an almost religious awe. This attitude is also reflected in the adulation of public figures such as those involved in sport and entertainment.

With the Spanish Conquest (1519-21) an autochthonous *mestizo* culture emerges and documented history begins. Christianisation and Hispanisation started simultaneously with the landing of the first missionaries in 1523. The force of indigenous religiosity now shifted to the Catholic Church. The Spaniards offered the Indian one God but many images of Christ, the Virgin and a multitude of Saints to replace his displaced deities. Nowadays, 95 per cent of the population is Catholic.

The colonial art of Mexico is, then, a religious art, primarily architectural, and sumptuous in form; the sixteenth century offers more architectural experiments than any other period of colonial history. Great demands were made upon the painters of the day. As the thousands of parochial churches were built, paintings were needed for the walls and altars. A most distinctive style in architecture had developed by the eighteenth century: the term ultra-baroque (*churrigueresco*) is used to describe the complex, intricately ornamented style of churches and civic buildings.

After Mexican independence in 1821, an extensive popular art flourished. Lithography rapidly became the vehicle for popular expression, its peculiar technical qualities allowing it wide diffusion and establishing a tradition for using the graphic arts as a means of social and political commentary.

If colonial art was dominated by architecture, since the early twentieth century it is the painters, particularly the muralists, who have occupied a pre-eminent position in Mexican art and though the various movements began with strongly national themes, they have sought to express concepts that transcend the national. Literature no longer deals with the revolution but with characters and subjects that are universally applicable; music, too, has been transformed so that it belongs to no specific country.

Thus a tendency toward the cosmopolitan, which paradoxically blends with a tendency toward a nationalistic culture is, perhaps, the most characteristic aspect of modern Mexico's cultural environment.

5 GOVERNMENT AND POLITICS

The War of Independence from Spain began in 1810, and independence was won in 1821 followed in 1824 by a constitution, making Mexico a republic. For the next hundred years the country experienced social unrest, foreign invasion and revolution before the constitution of 1917 paved the way for social stability, and order was finally restored in 1920. Since then, although the political environment has been dominated by one party, the presidential succession has remained peaceful and the role of the army has decreased markedly. The nationalisation of the petroleum industry in 1938 initiated a movement toward greater economic autonomy. From 1945 onwards the population more than doubled, industrialisation increased and, today, social reforms continue in a political environment of relative tranquillity. Beginning with the election of Miguel Alemán Valdés in 1946, Mexico has had an unbroken line of civilian 'first magistrates'. José López Portillo was elected President in 1976 for a 6-year term.

The constitution of 1917 established Mexico as a representative, democratic and federal republic consisting of 31 states, each with its own constitution, governor and chamber of deputies, and a federal district (Mexico City), seat of the federal government. Provisions were made for independent executive, legislative and judicial branches based on the separation of powers.

Legislature is bicameral with a Chamber of Deputies and a Senate elected by direct popular vote every 3 and 6 years respectively. There is one deputy for every

250,000 inhabitants; each state must have at least 2 deputies. Each state elects 2 senators and 2 more are seated from the federal district; senatorial terms run concurrent with the presidential term.

Supreme executive authority is vested in one individual, the President, who is elected to serve a single 6-year-term, and can never be re-elected. He appoints members of his cabinet, the government of the federal district which consists of Mexico City and several neighbouring small towns and villages, the Attorney General, the judges of the higher courts and diplomatic officials. He also appoints, with the Senate's approval, the senior officers of the Army, Navy and Air Force.

The President works through 16 ministries and 2 departments known as the 'decentralised sector', which includes almost 800 quasi-state companies and a number of decentralised agencies or bureaux.

Judicial power at the federal level is exercised by the Supreme Court of Justice in conjunction with district and circuit courts. Each state has its own superior court, as well as civil and criminal courts. At a lower level there are mixed 'magistrates' courts. Civil and penal codes are based principally on Roman law. A Mexican legal innovation is the *Juicio de Amparo* (a form of injunction), which makes it possible for a citizen to contest any law or executive act that violates any individual's constitutionally guaranteed rights. The *Amparo* is also used in adjudicating conflicts between state and federal statutes.

The federal judiciary is independent and can restrain even the President. In practice, however, the Supreme Court seems to take its cues largely from executive policy.

The structure of state and municipal governments is similar to that of the federal government. Regulated under the provisions of their own constitutions, each state may levy taxes and legislate under specific conditions. All powers not delegated to the federal government are reserved to the states.

The political system can be described as an 'elective system' with one dominant party. The President wields extensive power consonant with his central role in political and administrative matters. Close ties with an influential President confer a unique position on the major political party, the PRI (Institutional Revolutionary Party). Although there are three other viable officially recognised parties, the PRI has not lost a single presidential, gubernatorial or senatorial contest since its creation in 1929. The importance of the PRI depends on its encompassing all the larger popular organisations of the country: workers, farmers and the professional unions.

The President generally obtains a majority vote on bills he initiates, since over 80 per cent of the Chamber are members of the PRI.

The opposition parties have up to now played a relatively unimportant role in Mexico's political life. Only the PAN (Partido Acción Nacional) has offered any competition - although without actually threatening the hegemony of the PRI. However, on 1 September 1977, the President of the Republic, José López Portillo, in his first State of the Union message introduced a Reform Bill aimed at creating a more open electoral system. The Bill would guarantee the rights of political parties which were already registered and give minority parties increased access to the means of stable growth within the system.

This Bill will greatly change Mexican politics by increasing the number of parties which are significantly influential from 4 to 11. The parties expected to benefit from the reform are: the Mexican Communist Party (PCM), Mexican Workers' Party (PMT), Socialist Workers' Party (PST), Revolutionary Workers' Party (PRT), Democratic Mexican Party (PDM), Socialist Revolutionary Party (PSR) and the Left Communist Union (UIC).

Outside the potential parties as such, opposition exists in the form of groups in the commercial and industrial sectors which lobby through their trade associations and guilds. Students are also active politically and exert significant pressure.

6 ECONOMY

Over the last 35 years, in contrast to most developing countries, Mexico has sharply reduced the degree of foreign control in key sectors of its economy while still maintaining overall national growth. The state has assumed control of development of banks, railways, oil and heavy petrochemical and electric power industries including their distribution systems. It also has reduced foreign interests in mining and in important manufacturing businesses. At the same time, Mexico has recorded the highest sustained pace of economic growth in Latin America. The gross national product (GNP) more than doubled between 1950 and 1965 and, in the 1965-74 period the real increase in GNP averaged 6.5 per cent a year.

Fluctuations in the international monetary system have been especially marked since the early 1970s, producing possibly the worst crisis suffered by the market economy countries since World War II. They have particularly affected the under-developed nations which do not export petroleum. Mexico falls into this category and the GNP growth rate decreased by approximately 4.5 per cent in the year 1975-6.

There was rapid public investment to offset the slowdown in private investment and to stimulate production. Federal investment climbed 307 per cent in 1970-5, from 22.6 billion pesos to nearly 92 billion. Some 35 per cent of the total went to industrial development; 16 per cent to agriculture and fishing; 23 per cent to transport and communications and the remainder to social welfare, defence and administration.

This outlay seemed to reactivate the Mexican economy, although it inevitably put a strain on the balance of payments. Massive imports of raw materials and machinery, in spite of extensive import substitutions, more than doubled the trade deficit between 1960 and 1970. This deficit increased in 1970-5 when imports grew 183.31 per cent and exports 122.93 per cent.

TABLE 1

	(million US dollars)					
	1970	1971	1972	1973	1974	1975
Imports	2319	2250	2718	3813	6056	6580
Exports	1282	1365	1674	2070	2850	2858

Source: DGE, Secretaría de Industria y Comercio (Ministry of Industry and Commerce)

This deficit, plus inflation which averaged 20 per cent annually during 1971-6, forced the government to float the peso which had artificially retained its value since 1954 and which was classified by the International Monetary Fund as one of the world's reserve currencies. However, Mexico's per capita income has increased from US $661 in 1970 to US $1307 in 1975 as GNP growth has always surpassed population growth. This growth in the Mexican economy over the past four decades has benefited regions and classes very unequally. Mexico's market economy, although regulated by the State, has favoured the city over the country; the northern and central states, including Mexico City (federal district), as opposed to the southern states; and the upper and middle classes as opposed to rural and urban workers. So by 1963, 60 per cent of the Mexican population, comprising the lowest socio-economic strata, received only 21.5 per cent of all personal income as opposed to 24.6 per cent in 1950. Although contemporary economic policies are aimed towards economic growth and a more egalitarian distribution of economic benefits and developmental gains, these policies have not improved the situation. By 1973, the average income of 5 per cent of the population was 32 times higher than that of 20 per cent of the population. In general terms, 50 per cent of the population received only 15 per cent of the total income.

The instability of the manual labour market has had a depressing effect on urban salaries. At the same time, the inability of the industrial sector to increase employment opportunities explains the high rate of urban and rural under-employment.

The national budget for 1977 totalled US $28,014,727,000 (1 peso = $0.24). The main expenditures were on quasi-state industries and enterprises (US $13,754,318,000); the public debt (US $3,674,545,000); and education (US $2,716,181,800). The sum for education is one of the highest over the last 25 years and 8 times larger than that assigned to national defence.

This budget clearly indicates the present policy of the Mexican government to increase state participation in the mixed economy, since 49 per cent of the total budget is now allocated to quasi-state companies. In 1976, for the first time, public investment surpassed private investment.

7 EDUCATION

Since 1921, primary education has been free and compulsory. The outlay for schooling in 1976 was 20.4 per cent of the national budget or 2.8 per cent of the GNP. However, the demand for sufficient classrooms and adequate teaching staff is still not met. These needs are only accentuated by the high birth rate.

According to 1970-6 statistics, there are only enough pre-primary schools for an average of 10 per cent of the population in that age group. Of a total of 12 million pupils enrolled in primary schools, moreover, 1 million fail the examinations and 43 out of every 100 pupils drop out because they must earn a living or contribute to the family income. Only 700,000 out of every million primary school graduates move on to secondary school. This figure shrinks to approximately 450,000 pupils in the second and third years. Preparatory and vocational schools have places for more than 710,000 students and total university enrolment numbers 530,000 students.

Adult illiteracy in 1970 was 28.3 per cent with more than 10 million people over fifteen unable to read; 59 per cent of these illiterates live in rural areas, 41 per cent in urban areas. These alarming figures have forced the Government and education authorities to increase the number of widespread literacy campaigns. The Plan Nacional de Educación para Adultos (National Plan for Adult Primary Education) was initiated at the end of 1975 to replace the then current Plan de Once Años (Eleven-Year Plan), which was not satisfactory. The National Plan offers basic reading skills as well as primary and open secondary courses. During the 1970-6 period, an annual average of 110,000 adults attended literacy centres at the primary level and 300,000 at the secondary level.

8 TELECOMMUNICATIONS

A federal entity, the Secretaría de Comunicaciones y Transportes (SCT, Ministry of Communications and Transport), founded in 1959, provides and operates all telecommunications services, both public and specialised.

The Communications Section of the SCT is divided into three departments: telecommunications, postal services and telegraph services. All must submit major questions of policy to the Under-Secretary; final decisions are taken by the Minister in conjunction with the President.

A wide range of radio communication links provides telephone, telex, broadcasting, maritime communications and other telecommunication services. The federal microwave network currently extends to 13,300 km and has 56 terminal stations and 221 repeaters. When possible, Mexico uses this network to communicate, for example, with Guatemala, Belize and other countries as far south as Costa Rica. The same facilities are used for communicating with the United States of America and Canada. However, when it is technically advisable to use satellite communications, Mexico uses the INTELSAT service via the earth station at Tulancingo.

The National Centre of Operations, located in Torre Central de Telecomunicaciones (Telecommunications Control Tower) of the SCT, distributes and processes all the television signals through the federal microwave network.

The quasi-state enterprise Teléfonos de Mexico, also under the supervision of the SCT's Department of Telecommunications, is responsible for the telephone service. TDM is rapidly expanding and was recently incorporated into the international direct dialling network. There are now 3.1 million telephones, which means approximately 6 telephones for every 100 inhabitants.

Telecommunications are also being actively used in the development of data- and memory-bank archive services, facsimile and teleconferencing. The third department of the SCT's Communications Section is the Telégrafos Nacionales (National Telegraph Service). This cheap and reliable service is a major benefit to Mexico's 12.5 million rural inhabitants. Priority has also been given to this economic group by the department charged with postal services.

There is a broadcasting section of the SCT whose specific function is to regulate the technical and legal aspects of transmission. One of its subsections, the Dirección General de Concesiones y Permisos (Department of Concessions and Permits), allocates frequencies to broadcasters in accordance with international agreements and grants operational concessions to private enterprise.

9 MASS MEDIA

Press

Mexico's printed media operate under the sixth and seventh constitutional guarantees of freedom of expression governed by the Ley de Imprenta (Publishing Law) which protects the rights to inform and the right to privacy. The great majority of publications are privately owned; some conservative social pressures have resulted in a degree of criticism of the Government and its policies on print media. Perhaps this situation is partly due to the fact that, though there is no official censorship, all the paper required by publishing companies is produced and imported by the quasi-state enterprise, PIPSA.

In 1974, Mexico had 223 major daily newspapers, of which 27 were located in Mexico City, including 'Excelsior', considered one of the most important newspapers in the Spanish-speaking world. However, in spite of its prestige, 'Excelsior' does not enjoy the circulation of the city's more popular newspapers.

The newspapers with a nationwide circulation are especially important in the formation of public opinion; in 1974 5,700,000 copies were distributed daily to 10,943,396 families or 1 copy for every 2 households.

A tradition of Mexican newspapers is the *gacetilla* - editorial material paid for by those who insert it. It still exists but is less widespread than formerly.

Of the numerous news, literary and other specialised magazines, only 146, chiefly 'true confession', women's and sports magazines, have significant sales. They total about 20 million copies a month.

Cinema

The Mexican film industry reached its peak during World War II; by the 1950s the industry was in crisis. Its old established stars and time-tested plots could no longer hope to yield the returns that they had so long enjoyed from their Latin American outlets. The average annual production of 100 films dropped to less than 50 in 1961. One cause was television, which was introduced in 1950.

In order to fight the slump and keep the national cinema alive, the government took over the studios, distributing agencies, and most of the theatres. All the sections that make up the commercial film industry are now affiliated with the Banco Nacional Cinematográfico (National Film Bank), which has absorbed the losses of past years and now subsidises film production. The Bank is set up with sufficient funds to finance the studios (and keep them functioning), to provide the necessary capital for distribution, to construct or acquire theatres and to sustain advertising and promotional programmes. Directly or indirectly, the Bank provides 90 per cent of the industry's overall financing.

In the 6-year period 1970-6, a total of 346 films were produced and two new state agencies were created to stimulate and control production. Another recent innovation was the establishment of the Centro de Capacitación Cinematográfico (Film Training Centre) to serve as a training ground for young film-makers.

Chapter 2

THE ADVENT AND DEVELOPMENT OF BROADCASTING IN MEXICO

1 RADIO: THE BEGINNINGS (1921-9)

The first radio broadcasts in Mexico began on an experimental basis in the latter half of 1921. These pioneer transmissions originated in the federal district and in the City of Monterrey and were soon followed by others in the northern states.

It was not until 1923 that the Mexican federal government authorised the first commercial stations. From that time on, the industry gathered momentum. The same year three amateur 'radio clubs' merged into a professional league, the Liga Central Mexicana (Central Mexican League), laying the foundations for the influential Cámera Nacional de la Industria de Radio y Televisión (National Chamber of the Radio and Television Industry), an organisation representing all commercial broadcasting stations. One of the initial activities of the League was to make proposals for a regulatory framework to 'contain' the broadcasting industry. Among their proposals was the recommendation that from 7-10 pm no government or public service transmission should be aired, but that the time should be reserved for commercial use. These suggested guidelines illustrate the early institutionalisation of broadcasting as a primarily commercial medium.

The infant radio industry was strongly influenced by the North American broadcasting paradigm which had been closely studied by Mexican entrepreneurs once they recognised the new medium as a profitable area for investment.

The 1920s were years of great political turbulence and the armed struggles among the various revolutionary factions inevitably had grave economic consequences. The government, preoccupied with survival and reconstruction as well as shaping a viable foreign policy, was too busy to pay much attention to the radio industry. The advent of commercial radio was therefore not directly affected by government policies.

Programming in the early years consisted principally of news, popular music and advertising. The close link between radio and the press at that time was reflected by the substantial amount of news programmes on stations whose owners were also newspaper publishers.

By 1929 there were seventeen long-wave stations. Two were state-owned. One of them, founded in 1924 by the Secretaría de Educación Publica (Ministry of Public Education), began transmission with the inaugural speech of President Plutarco Elías Calles and closed down in 1940, to be reopened as Radio Educación some years later.

Aside from this tentative participation of the state as broadcaster, the government was hardly aware of the possibilities of broadcasting and regulatory norms were almost nonexistent. The only significant constitutional edict relating to broadcasting was the Ley de Comunicaciones Eléctricas (Electrical Communications Law) of 1926 (see chapter 3) which dealt with a few technical aspects and which was supplemented by additional legislative enactments in the 1930s. Thus almost all initial decisions pertaining to programming content and the operations of radio stations were made by private enterprise.

The institutional development of the system

The major impetus to the development and expansion of the radio industry came in the 1930s, with consequences at both the quantitative and qualitative levels. The Government began to grant stable concessions to radio stations in place of the precarious annual permits of the past. In 1932, ten new commercial long-wave stations began transmission in Mexico City along with twenty stations in the interior's urban centres. The majority of the stations outside the capital were concentrated in the border cities, perhaps due to a desire to take advantage of an audience that had become accustomed to the USA's broadcasts. By 1940 there were ten long-wave commercial stations; this number was more than doubled, reaching 95 per cent of the states and totalling 205 by 1950.

As the medium expanded, competition among the commercial stations to capture mass audiences grew and programming became more rigid and more structured. The substantial advertising revenues allowed radio managements to present an increasing amount of live entertainment, specifically in the areas of comedy, drama, folk music and sports. Another innovation of that era with initial and lasting impact was the serialised melodrama, the *radio novela* or soap-opera which became enormously popular during those years of limited literacy, and took on the status of folk literature. Many of these established programmes were used later as springboards into television.

Emilio Azcárraga Vidaurreta, a distributor and affiliate of the Radio Corporation of America (RCA) in Mexico, played a major part in the promotion of radio. He had enormous confidence in the potential of the new medium as a delivery system for his recorded music, invested heavily and established himself in the vanguard of commercial radio. In 1930 he inaugurated XEW, 'The Voice of Latin America', which was affiliated to the National Broadcasting Corporation (NBC), the radio division of RCA in the United States. XEW was the first station to receive an operating concession from the government and rapidly became the bell-wether of the industry.

The next step was the creation of networks. Azcárraga and NBC began to affiliate other stations of the interior to their XEW transmitter. By 1938 NBC had 14 affiliates. XEQ, inaugurated that same year and affiliated to the Columbia Broadcasting System (CBS), expanded to 17 stations by 1945. Besides these two large networks, CYB, backed by French capital, was operating during the 1930s and the early 1940s with 20 stations throughout the country.

Radio Cadena Continental, founded in 1942, linked ten stations in Mexico City at certain hours, thereby saturating the 'dial' with the same programmes. About 90 per cent of network radio was concentrated in the central and northern states of the country. This pattern clearly reflects the unequal socio-economic distribution from region to region, mentioned in the previous chapter.

After 1945, XEW and XEQ expanded more slowly because their management's major efforts were directed toward the introduction and development of television. However, Radio Mil, created in 1942, offered strong competition and eventually expanded into five stations broadcasting exclusively in Mexico City. Each participating station was autonomously programmed but joined the pool for shared news programmes.

One of the last commercial stations of importance to emerge during this era was XEX, founded in 1947. The station was later acquired by Rómulo O'Farrill Sr, a dominant figure in Mexican newspaper publishing. Under his management, XEX became a 'radio-journal' with the emphasis on news and current affairs. Together, XEX and Radio Mil stimulated higher standards of broadcast journalism and saw the introduction of professional news services.

The state's role as a broadcaster remained low-key throughout the 1930s and 1940s. Nevertheless, 2 government stations of particular significance did begin to operate during those years: the Ministry of Education's station, and a station organised by the Partido Nacional Revolucionario (now the PRI), the first 'official' party in Mexico and also, in 1931, the first political party to have its own station. Programming consisted chiefly of material on party activities and policies, leavened with talks on art and literature. In 1948, by Presidential decree, the station was handed over to the private sector.

Another facet of state participation is Radio Gobernación, created in 1937. This production organisation is responsible for *La Hora Nacional* ('The National Hour'), a magazine show carried simultaneously on Sundays by all radio stations in the nation. Produced at commercial radio facilities in Mexico City, 'The National Hour' serves as the government's official communication outlet. A typical programme will offer a mixture of political information, dramatisations of relevant history and a fair amount of folk and popular music.

Broadcasting policies and regulation lagged behind. Government activity consisted solely of responses to the much more energetic private initiatives. However, in 1936 a piece of legislation was passed which did have major repercussions. The Ley de Cámaras de Comercio e Industria (Law of Chambers of Commerce and Industry) obliged all persons and entities engaged in industry or trade to become members of their respective 'chambers'. This law enabled the government to group similar enterprises, including radio stations, into a manageable organisation that could and would deal with the state.

Finally, in 1940, a landmark in legislation was enacted

giving the federal government exclusive regulatory jurisdiction over broadcasting, congruent with previous legislation. Under the Ley de Vías Generales de Comunicación (Law of General Communications Means) the Ministry of Communications and Public Works was authorised to grant concessions and permits, to classify and prescribe the general functions of stations, and to establish regulations concerning technical matters. A novel section of the Law made the Ministry responsible for regulating advertising rates. The new legislation did not make any attempt to interfere with programme cortent and this area remained in the hands of station owners.

By the late 1940s the industry had reached maturity. Radio was no longer a sideshow but had become a full-time profession demanding high degrees of specialisation in programming, production and journalism.

The advent of television has not diminished radio vitality. The industry, re-structured, has grown at a pace consonant with the increase in population and the expansion of Mexican markets. During the last two decades new networks and stations, such as Radio Fórmula and Radio Centro, have appeared and flourished. The first FM station was introduced in 1953 and public response had been good enough to occasion a steady increase in FM coverage. By 1977 there were 584 AM stations broadcasting and 110 FM stations.

As in other countries with both radio and TV, Mexico's radio does not compete with television for the same audience. By programming on the principle of 'audience segmentation', radio has shifted the emphasis from the broad-spectrum formats to more narrowly focused programmes aimed at specific 'target' audiences which, in turn, constitute viable markets for explicit sponsorship. A station may specialise in 'youth' programming, in 'ethnic' content, in nostalgia, in classical music. In short, each station isolates and attempts to serve a clearly defined audience. This factor, together with the use of radio to supply background 'noise' to combat solitude, and its use at times and in places inappropriate to video entertainment (vehicles, offices, factories, etc.), assures the medium a secure future.

2 TELEVISION: THE BEGINNINGS (1950-60)

In 1950, Mexico became the sixth country in the world to establish commercial television. The year takes on special significance when seen as the beginning of a period of burgeoning national industrial development rooted in political stability.

In contrast to the time when radio was established, the government was in 1950 in a position to take a lively interest in the medium and an active role in its growth. When, in 1947, both Azcárraga and O'Farrill had plans to introduce television and asked for concessions from the government, the then President of the republic, Miguel Alemán Valdés (1946-52), appointed a high-level Commission to survey the television industries taking shape abroad, particularly in the United States and Great Britain. The Commission's directive was to indicate to the government which of the current patterns of television broadcasting would be best suited to Mexico.

Two obvious contenders were the relatively free-wheeling US model of private enterprise and the Western European systems of broadcasting models which have a tighter constitutional relationship with government. The federal government's decision was in favour of development through private enterprise regulated by federal agencies. Investigation led the Commissioners to feel that, lacking adequate resources and in the absence of a suitable infrastructure, it would be folly to launch an extensive full-scale government television operation. The Commission also believed that the population simply was neither interested in nor prepared for the kind of educative, worthy programming produced by the BBC and other European organisations.

The result was a plan providing for a nationwide web of television channels operating primarily in a framework of private enterprise with provisions for gradually implemented government facilities appearing and functioning on a small scale. Frequencies were allotted and reserved to the state for later use as channels for educational and cultural programming.

From the outset Mexican television has been owned, operated, and financed by Mexican nationals. The 1940 Ley de Vías Generales de Comunicación (Law of General Communications Means) stipulated that no foreigner could own a broadcasting channels. However, much of the technical equipment for television was imported, particularly from the United States. Numerous programmes were also bought from the United States in the early days; mostly feature films and 'dubbed' film series. These imports were counter-balanced at first by live productions and then, in the late 1950s, by the introduction of videotape, using locally taped shows.

The earliest television station was Channel 4, founded by the publishing magnate Rómulo O'Farrill Sr, in late 1950. Its first major broadcast was the Executive State of the Union Message of the Alemán administration. Shortly after this, Channel 2, the Azcárraga flagship station, began sporadic transmissions. Then, in early 1952, Televicentro was inaugurated. Its 10 studios and ample equipment contrasted strongly with Channel 4's single studio.

A third competitor appeared on the scene in late 1952, when Guillermo González Camarena inaugurated Channel 5 with a small but well-equipped studio complex. Camarena, an electronics engineer, had been conducting experiments in television since 1925. As a technical pioneer in the television field, by 1940 he had successfully exhibited working models of transmitters and receivers for colour broadcasting. However, Camarena was not in a position to compete with the vast resources of the trans-national companies already battling to dominate the colour business.

The 3 channels, all located in Mexico City, accepted a modus vivendi of commercial competition. Continually vying for the rights to broadcast soccer matches, bullfights, baseball games and other special events, they inevitably inflated the costs. In 1955, therefore, due to the limited economic possibilities of the market, the 3 independents united to form Telesistema Mexicano (TSM). This concentration of resources and joint operation seemed to be the best way for the industry to survive and grow. The centralised management of TSM was in a good position to provide diverse programming directed to different segments of the market on each of its channels. Channel 2 specialised in variety shows, situation comedies, drama and game shows. Its news coverage was international and included special events of universal significance. From the beginning, almost all of Channel 2's programming was of Mexican origin.

Channel 4 showed *telenovelas* (soap-operas), foreign

feature films, Mexican-oriented news and, principally, sports. Channel 5's programming was entirely composed of children's programmes and animated cartoons and foreign material such as action adventure series and feature films.

The state's participation began in 1958 when the government assigned Channel 11 to the Secretaría de Educación Publica (Ministry of Public Education) which in turn gave the concession to the Institute Politécnico Nacional (National Polytechnical Institute). From the beginning, the channel has operated with a limited budget provided by the Ministry. It is not allowed to finance itself through advertising. Production and technical standards have therefore been no more than adequate. Even today, transmission power is limited and the channel is seen in only a few homes.

1960 saw the introduction of the crucial Ley Federal de Radio y Televisión (Federal Law of Radio and Television). For the first time the government took action to participate as a broadcaster through the channels that were operated by private enterprise. It also began to regulate programme content. This law will be fully discussed in Chapter 3.

The institutional development of the system (1961-77)

The early 1960s were years of consolidation for commercial television. The rapid spread of videotape recording encouraged stations to expand throughout the country. TSM, with no competition in Mexico City, quickly expanded to the provinces where it competed with the new television channels. At the same time, Teleprogramas de Mexico, founded in 1955 to export recorded programmes and affiliated to TSM, now extended its markets into the rest of the Spanish-speaking world through the use of videotapes. Another TSM affiliate, Teleprogramas Acapulco, was created in 1966 to mass produce *telenovelas* and to explore new potentials of the format. The company was headed by Miguel Alemán Velasco.

The country's deep involvement in the XIX Olympiad held in Mexico in 1968 had a vital impact on the television industry. Colour television transmissions had begun in 1967 in preparation for the games; television networks established near-blanket coverage of the entire republic; and the government constructed a high-capacity microwave network between Mexico City and the United States border, and built a satellite ground station.

The first television station in the provinces had been installed by TSM in 1951 near Mexico City to relay Channel 2's programming. A few local stations had emerged, most of which transmitted TSM programming together with some local production. The expansion of television in the provinces really got under way in the 1960s when TSM installed the majority of its stations. But, with the advent of the microwave network, and in order to provide national television coverage of the Olympic Games, the majority of these stations were converted into repeaters. By 1968, there were 37. TSM became the first network in the country, principally with Channel 2's repeaters.

Competition in the provinces began for TSM in 1967 with the inauguration of Telecadena Mexicana's first three channels in capital cities of the north. Telecadena was founded in 1965 by film producer Manuel Barbachano Ponce. By the early 1970s it was operating 15 channels in the northern and central states. Each channel had one studio and black-and-white equipment, principally organised as a 'film chain'. Programming was made up chiefly of Mexican feature films, Peruvian *telenovelas*, North American and European series and a small amount of local production.

However, Telecadena slowly succumbed to financial pressures. One of the main causes of its eventual demise was the shortage of local advertising. Even regional advertisers preferred to have their publicity originated in Mexico City and then transmitted on a national network. By 1972 all of the 15 channels operating under Telecadena Mexicana had been affiliated to Channel 8 in Mexico City. However, when Telecadena Mexicana declared bankruptcy in late 1975, the government took possession of 8 of the 15 stations and assigned them as 'repeaters' to the state-owned Channel 13.

In Mexico City, the period of non-competition which followed the foundation of TSM came to an end in 1968, when Channel 8 went on the air. Channel 8, known as Televisión Independiente de México (TIM), was backed by a strong industrial group in the north. It competed across the board for the same audience which TSM served with its three channels. *Telenovelas*, musicals, variety shows and important sports events were again the subjects of fierce bidding.

Channel 13 also went on the air in 1968, as another commercial channel. It was managed by Corporación Mexicana de Radio y Televisión (CRMT), which had been founded by Francisco Aguirre, a radio entrepreneur whose group of stations was by the late 1960s successfully challenging the old-line radio networks that had flourished during the 1930s and the 1940s. Its coverage was limited to Mexico City's metropolitan area. Hoping to avoid head-on competition with both TSM and TIM, Channel 13 confined itself largely to re-runs of North American and other foreign films. Its ephemeral economic success was based on the competition's temporary weaknesses in local production and the over-intensive commercialisation of the time allotted to advertising. Plans to enlarge the channel's programming in 1971 by incorporating news along with quizzes, contests and audience participation shows were never realised. Aguirre divested himself of CMRT stock which was acquired by a quasi-state enterprise, Sociedad Mexicana de Crédito Industrial (SOMEX). By 1972, due to internal corporate problems, SOMEX became the sole owner of Channel 13.

In 1966, under the auspices of TSM, a cable television company called Cablevisión was organised in Mexico City. The station became operational in 1970. It served several Mexico City districts, reaching approximately 10,000 subscribers with Channels 7 and 10 and offering viewers improved reception of all local television channels.

From its inception, Channel 10 transmitted only North American programming picked up along the border with the United States and sent to Mexico City by microwave. In contrast, Channel 7 attempted some local programming. Live shows were produced in a small studio and a great many 'amateur' films were shown. But later this channel switched to a programme schedule similar to Channel 10's. Currently both channels are dominated by programmes picked up from the major US networks. News programmes, however, are produced locally. No such specific regulation exists in the Legal Code but, by analogy with the 'regular' over-the-air law, the cable operators do produce their own service.

Cablevisión inaugurated Telstar, Channel 20, as a new service to subscribers in the first quarter of 1977. Telstar feeds clients the time, weather, financial data, news and other useful viewer-oriented information during its broadcasting day.

Chapter 2

Apart from Cablevisión, there are 30 private cable companies serving 65 populated areas in the republic. These systems, which began to develop during the 1960s in the provinces, pick up the signals of the Mexico City channels as well as US programming in the case of the border towns. Several stations do have plans to undertake local production in the near future.

The federal government, in May 1972, took a significant step by creating Televisión Rural de México (TRM), decreed by Presidential fiat. As a government agency dependent on the Secretaría de Comunicaciones (Ministry of Communications and Transport) and since 1977, on the Secretaría de Gobernación (Ministry of the Interior), its prime mission was to provide telecasts to the marginal rural zones of the nation. It now transmits by microwave 8 hours of programming from the Telecommunications Control Tower to areas not covered by commercial television networks or Channel 13. In populated areas not yet incorporated into the microwave network, programmes are delivered in videocassettes.

Although TRM's programming will be described in more detail in Chapter 5, it should be noted here that, since TRM's main objective is to re-transmit television signals to marginal areas not reached by commercial channels, it does almost no production of its own. Its 8 hours of programming largely consist of material drawn from both commercial and government channels according to a selection made by TRM's Programming Council. The emphasis, however, is on programmes from the official channels.

The state entered into direct participation in the industry in 1972 by assuming control of Channel 13. During the summer of that year, commercial television was closely scrutinised and severely criticised by the government and by the national press. In Mexico, where a large portion of the population is either still illiterate or minimally schooled, competitive commercial broadcasting had, more and more, allowed its programming to decline to the level of the lowest common denominator in order to reach the broadest possible audience and to create ever higher ratings for pollsters and advertisers. Many critics, particularly educationalists, felt that the tendency was leading to warped perceptions and the dissemination of misinformation which, in turn, led to degraded public tastes. They also pointed out that an opportunity to use the airways 'pro bono publico' was being irretrievably lost by the present holders of the telecasting franchise.

Mexican commercial television reacted sharply to this hostile onslaught. Later, when the invective and polemic had died, the broadcasters began serious introspection. The inevitable conclusion was that, given Mexico's specific socio-economic realities, portions of the criticism were well-founded and something would have to be done. More pragmatically, the realisation that the government had effectively become a direct competitor convinced commercial management that operators like TSM and TIM simply did not have sufficient resources to go their separate ways and survive in competition with the government in the long haul. TSM and TIM voted to pool their forces. By the beginning of 1973, a 'confederation' of Channels 2, 4, 5 and 8, called Televisa, was functioning under joint administration.

The changes begun in 1972 have had a profound and lasting effect on the pattern of Mexican broadcasting. Televisa has become conscious of a public service role and a civic responsibility that it cannot safely ignore. In 1973 plans were carried out to implement a policy without precedent, a policy of cultural and educational programming. By 1977, according to Televisa's figures, 115 hours per week were devoted to this type of material on Televisa's 4 channels.

With similar realism, Channel 13 has abandoned its original determination to operate with almost no advertising and is stepping up efforts to become self-sufficient and financially sound through the sale of commercial time.

Chapter 3

BROADCASTING STRUCTURES AND REGULATORY FRAMES

As we have seen, the Mexican broadcasting industry underwent dynamic growth between 1932 and 1968 as the number of professional organisations, and transmission and reception facilities, greatly increased. The process relied to a great extent on strong individual entrepreneurs and the government's apparent lack of awareness of the considerable importance of the medium. It was disorganised and intuitive. There were very few general policies and regulatory codes. When such policies did exist, they lagged behind the actual development of the industry. The government did little more than react to the broadcasters' more energetic initiatives. The lack of public initiative was evident in the way the broadcasters saturated the biggest markets and hardly touched the rest of the country. The government did not establish a legislative framework for radio and television until 1960, when the first regulatory measures specifically applicable to broadcasting were taken.

Since that date, the government has become more and more involved in broadcasting. By the mid 1970s, it had a strong foothold in the industry, not only with regard to legislation but also through regulatory bodies and governmental agencies. By this time the government was also participating directly as the owner of important components of the telecommunications infrastructure and as a broadcaster.

1 ANTECEDENTS OF THE 1960 FEDERAL LAW OF RADIO AND TELEVISION

The first statute related to broadcasting was the Ley de Comunicaciones Electricas (Law of Electrical Communications) of 1926, which regulated 'telegraphy, radiotelegraphy, telephony, radio-telephony and any other electrical system of sound, signs or images, and of transmission and reception with or without wires'. This Law established some general principles that are still in force today, such as the federal government's exclusive regulatory jurisdiction over electrical communications, including broadcasting, and the ruling that franchises could be granted only to Mexican citizens. There were also injunctions against the transmission via electrical communications of messages that might threaten national security and international peace, offend existing laws or established customs, invade the right of privacy or incite to crime.

In 1931, the Ley de Vias Generales de Comunicacion y Medios de Transporte (Law of General Communications Means and Transport Means) was passed. For the first time commercial, experimental, and cultural broadcasting stations were defined and regulated. In a single enactment this Law embraced legislative material pertaining to electrical communications, railways, highways, bridges and the postal code. However, the following year, profound modifications brought the Ley de Vias Generales de Comunicacion (Law of General Communications Means) which, in turn, was amended by a 1940 law carrying the same name.

The 1940 Law of General Communications Means, in accordance with previous legislation, gave the federal government exclusive regulatory jurisdiction over broadcasting. It also authorised the Ministry of Communications and Public Works to grant concessions and permits, to classify stations in accordance with established categories, to determine their location and prescribe their general functions, to establish regulations pertaining to technical operation; and to modify or revoke concessions if, in the Ministry's judgment, the public interest should so require.

The Ministry was also made responsible for regulating the advertising rates charged by commercial stations. Stations were required to carry, free of charge, messages concerning ships and aircraft in distress, national defence and the maintenance of public order. Any federal government programmes that were rated as being 'official' were to be transmitted with a 50 per cent discount on the rate-card cost. The Ministry was given broad powers to demand the correction or improvement of station services; to suspend any service which was not up to standard; and

Chapter 3

to levy fines and inflict penalties for violation of regulations as defined by law.

The Law also emphasised that no foreigner could own or control a radio station; nor could ownership or control be transferred without the approval of the Ministry of Communications and Public Works.

With the rapid expansion of radio during the 1940s and television's introduction in the early 1950s, the 1940 Law soon became obsolete. The expansion of the concept of a 'common carrier' of radio telegraphic regulation to include broadcasting seriously jeopardized the development of radio and television, implementing restrictions and sanctions which were not consonant with broadcasting's true nature and social function. One of the major criticisms of the Law of General Communications Means was that it did not go far enough in its treatment of broadcasting, along with telecommunications and transport, as a public utility. The Law's attitude, it was said, did not adequately recognise broadcasting's peculiar social significance. In the late 1950s, a major study verified the necessity for a new statute to specifically cover the means of transmission and reception, and to make further development more compatible with the paramount interests of the nation. In 1959, Congress began to consider legislative reform.

2 1960 FEDERAL LAW OF RADIO AND TELEVISION

The result was the Federal Law of Radio and Television, passed in January 1960, and still in force. All parts of the 1940 Law were repealed or superseded, with the exception of one section relating to the installation of amateur radio stations. Although the major part of the earlier statute concerning broadcasting was absorbed by the 1960 Law, there were important changes and additions. The new Act emphasises the social significance of broadcasting, and states that the electromagnetic spectrum (broadcast frequencies) is part of an inalienable public domain and may be utilised only under permits or through franchises granted by the federal government.

Furthermore, since broadcasting stations operate in the public interest the state is obligated to monitor and regulate their contracts to fulfil a civic and social need. In order to carry out this social function, the Law declares that radio and television must: (a) provide programmes that enhance respect for moral principles, human dignity and family ties; (b) avoid programmes that interfere with the healthy development of children; (c) seek to raise the cultural level of the people, preserve their customs, traditions and characteristics, and enrich the values of Mexican nationality; and (d) strengthen democratic beliefs, national unity and the principles of international amity and cooperation.

In addition, the Law points out that the state not only has a regulatory mission, but must also exercise an important active role in the realisation of these moral and social goals. Thus it declares that the President, through government agencies, must promote programmes which contribute to the social and cultural welfare of the community. The state is also charged with the responsibility to provide facilities for broadcasting to foreign countries in order to promote commercial trade and tourism and to supply information about Mexican life and culture.

An important innovation embodied in the 1960 Law was the division of regulatory responsibilities among various Ministries. Previous legislation gave wide regulatory authority over broadcasting to the President and to the Ministry of Communications and Public Works. In 1958 the Ministry of Communications and Public Works was abolished, and its functions taken over by the Ministry of Communications and Transport and the Ministry of Public Works. Under the current Law, the allocation and assignment of frequencies for station operation is the responsibility of the Ministry of Communications and Transport. It also grants, modifies or revokes concessions, franchises and permits; intervenes in the rental, sale or other transactions that affect the ownership of stations; and in general concerns itself with the regulation of technical operations.

In the past, advertising rates were determined by the government so that no change could be affected without the approval of the Communications Ministry. The present Law is less rigid. By retaining, to some extent, the common carrier concept, it was made mandatory that the Ministry of Communications and Transport fix the minimum advertising rate but broadcasters are permitted to charge more according to market demand.

The Ministry of the Interior has important powers over radio and television programmes. It acts as a 'watchdog' to see that the media do not violate the right to privacy, offend personal and moral dignity or attack or infringe the rights of third parties, provoke crime or disturb the peace or public order.

The same Ministry was made responsible for carrying out article 59 of the Law which states that every day all broadcasting stations must transmit at least 30 minutes of programming, either in one block or in segments, that has an educational, cultural and social orientation. The staff of the Ministry of the Interior prepares these programmes and makes them available to radio and television stations, which must broadcast them free of charge. The rationale behind this article is the idea that the airwaves are publicly owned, that the stations use them for profit and that they are therefore obliged to compensate the community by providing free broadcast time for the government to use in the interests of that commonweal.

The 1960 Law reflects the increasing concern of the government to improve education, particularly in the areas of literacy, technical, industrial and agricultural instruction as well as in the area of cultural themes. Under statutory mandate, the Ministry of Public Education (SEP) is charged with promoting the wider and more effective use of radio and television for educational purposes. Subsections of article 11 state that the Ministry shall: (a) promote and organise teaching through radio and television; (b) promote and broadcast programmes of a cultural and civic interest; (c) protect the rights of authors; (d) issue certificates of accreditation to announcers, commentators and other on-air personnel employed by stations and (e) with the exception of matters of copyright infringement, inform the Ministry of the Interior of all violations of requirements in this article, so that appropriate sanctions may be applied.

In addition the Ministry is responsible for the selection of the personnel who prepare and present its educational broadcasts. The municipalities, labour unions, agrarian groups and other organisations that participate are required to install, in adequate locations and with appropriate equipment, a sufficient number of receivers for the local community. The Ministry is also responsible for the creation of radio and television schools.

Under article 12 of the Federal Law of Radio and Television, provision is made for the Ministry of Health and Welfare (SSA) to promote the education of the public in the areas of nutrition, health and hygiene. The Ministry also supervises and authorises the contents of commercials that concern the practice of medicine or related activities as well as the texts used in advertising food, drinks, pharmaceutical products, insecticides, beauty preparations, therapeutic devices or anything marketed for the treatment and cure of disease or the promotion of health.

An important portion of the 1960 Law deals with programme content. To begin with, article 58 states that there shall be no 'prior' censorship of any broadcast material. It guarantees that freedom of expression and the right of reception shall not be curtailed or subject to judicial or administrative inquiry. However, this freedom is regulated by statutory provision of both a 'positive' and a 'negative' nature.

Some of the 'positive' provisions have already been mentioned. They include the requirement to broadcast the government's 30 minutes of programming; the priority that must be given to official bulletins relating to national security or defence, or in the interest of public order; the obligation to make available the necessary facilities for network broadcasting of urgent messages to the nation at the request of the President or of the Ministry of the Interior; the demand for a reasonable balance between advertising and general programming; and the requirement for a warning at the beginning of all programmes designated as unsuitable for children.

Other provisions state that programmes must give expression to and stimulate artistic values. Only the Spanish language may be used in broadcasts, unless special permission is obtained from the Ministry of the Interior (in which case, a Spanish version, in full or summarised, must be provided before transmission). Information about political, social and cultural matters of public importance, along with sports coverage, must be included in daily programming.

The 'negative' provisions prohibit broadcasts which may corrupt the Spanish language, violate the accepted customs of the community, encourage anti-social behaviour, denigrate national heroes, offend commonly-held religious beliefs or discriminate on grounds of race or colour.

It is not only illegal to broadcast messages contrary to the security of the state or against public order, it is also against the law to broadcast programmes from a foreign country without prior authorisation from the Ministry of the Interior. It is also understood that any publicity, promotion or solicitation for centres of vice is forbidden; as is the dissemination of any fraudulent or misleading advertising. There are restrictions on advertisements of alcoholic beverages: 'hard sell' is not allowed when the beverage is more than 20° proof. Minors may not be shown in the commercials; nor may any drinking, actual or simulated. There are time limits, too. No message for an alcoholic beverage may be aired before 10 pm, and tobacco may not be advertised in children's slots.

'Fiscal time'

The 1960 Law made provision for the government to use broadcasting time on commercial stations in accordance with the conditions outlined in articles 59, 60 and 62. These periods can be categorised as 'legal time'. However, a Decree issued in July 1969 has further accentuated the government's participation in broadcasting through the employment of what can be called 'fiscal time'. This idea originated in a December 1968 Presidential Decree pertaining to the Ley de Ingresos de la Federacion para el Ejercicio Fiscal (the Federal Tax and Internal Revenue Law) which states that a special tax would be imposed on all services declared by law to be of public interest, using media or channels authorised as franchises pertaining to the public domain. The tax amounts to 25 per cent of the total gross income of the company engaged in these services.

In the face of this Decree, which would severely hamper the economic development of radio and television, broadcasters proposed to the government that they paid the tax not in cash but in the form of broadcasting time made available to the state. The government accepted this compromise because it required more broadcasting time and in July 1969 issued a Presidential Decree authorising the Treasury and Ministry of Public Credit to charge a 25 per cent tax or, in lieu of this, a levy of 12.5 per cent of each station's daily broadcasting time to be used exclusively by the government. This Decree also declared that the government's daily transmission time is not cumulative and that if the state did not use its time, the concessionaire must fill the time and not interrupt the continuity of his schedule.

The government's broadcasting time should be proportionally and equally distributed through the total transmission hours of the radio or television station, but in such a manner as to avoid jeopardizing the economic stability of the station or upsetting the characteristics of its programming policy.

Government agencies regulating broadcasting

The Consejo Nacional de Radio y Televisión (National Council of Radio and Television) was established by the 1960 Law as a coordinating agency attached to the Ministry of the Interior. As prescribed by the Law, membership is made up of a representative from the Ministries of Public Education, of Communications and Transport, and of Health and Welfare, plus two additional 'management' members from the broadcast industry and two 'workers' in that industry.

According to article 91, the Council's duties are: (a) to promote and organise those broadcasts ordered by the President of the republic; (b) to serve as a consultative body to the President; (c) to improve the moral, cultural, artistic and social levels of broadcasting; (d) to have knowledge of and make decisions regarding matters submitted to the Council for study and opinion by the Ministries and Departments of the federal government and by institutions, agencies or persons concerned with radio and television.

This agency sees that all stations carry the official programming, and levies fines when they do not. Fines are set by the statute.

In order to make fuller use of the 12.5 per cent of time at its disposal, the government created the Comisión de Radiodifusión (Broadcasting Commission) in August 1969. The Commission has permanent members from the Ministries of the Interior, Treasury and Public Credit and Communications and Transport. One representative from the Ministry of Public Education and another from Health and Welfare are appointed as special members who sit on the board only when the issues treated are in their direct competence.

The Commission's specific functions are to determine the programming to be produced for use in the 12.5 per cent 'fiscal time' available as well as to arrive at transmission schedules with the stations. In television, according to official figures, the Commission produced 4,200 hours in 1974, 4,400 in 1975 and 5,600 in 1976.

In December 1970 the Subsecretaria de Radiodifusion (Under-Ministry of Broadcasting) was created as a dependency of the Ministry of Communications and Transport. Its objectives were to absorb all the functions allotted to the Ministry of Communications and Transport in the 1960 Federal Law of Radio and Television. In addition, the Subsecretaria de Radiodifusion was made responsible for the actual production of all the radio and television programmes that the Comision de Radiodifusion decided were to be aired during the 12.5 per cent broadcasting time accepted by the Government. A further obligation was to coordinate operations of the TRM network created in 1972.

Since January 1977, a totally new administrative reform has been taking place. A new agency, attached to the Ministry of the Interior, has been created. It is called Direccion General de Radio, Television y Cinematografia (RTC) and has taken over the functions which, in the past, were carried out by the Subsecretaria de Radiodifusion, which is now in the process of being dismantled.

In general terms, the objective of the creation of RTC is to unite the efforts and responsibilities which were formerly dispersed among various government agencies. The most significant task accomplished was the integration of the departments of the ex-Subsecretaria de Radiodifusion. The departments now integrated into the RTC are Research and Development, Engineering, Production and Television Rural de México (TRM). The only department left under the roof of the Ministry of Communications and Transport is that of Concessions and Permits. These changes may imply the modification, in the very near future, of the 1960 Federal Law of Radio and Television - particularly in regard to the regulatory powers assigned to each Ministry.

In order to carry out its functions, the RTC has six main operational divisions: (a) planning; (b) television; (c) radio; (d) cinema; (e) Presidential communications and (f) administration. All are under the General Director of RTC who reports directly to the Minister of the Interior.

The Department of Planning has the following functions: to carry out research on an overall framework for the development of policies regarding the national radio, television and cinema industries; to propose, coordinate and evaluate the implementation of the policies established by the RTC; to carry out studies of the technical, social and financial feasibility of the plans, programmes, projects and activities of each division of RTC; and periodically to evaluate the results obtained in the implementation of the programmes carried out by RTC.

The Departments of Radio and Television are responsible for developing legislation in regard to their respective medium in those matters that directly concern the Ministry of the Interior. In accordance with the programming policy of the 12.5 per cent 'fiscal time' established by the Comision de Radiodifusion, these departments must determine the programmes and establish transmission timetables. The Department of Television supervises the operations of TRM and participates in its Programming Council.

The Department of Presidential Communications was brought into being to coordinate the dissemination of official government information and to avoid duplication, contradictions and the misuse of resources; common abuses in the past. The function of this department is to keep the nation informed about the activities carried out by the President of the republic and about the public sector in general. It coordinates the information, publicity and public relations of the public sector and plans, and implements civic and public service campaigns on radio and television supporting the activities of the federal government.

Chapter 4

COMMERCIAL AND NON-COMMERCIAL RADIO

1 COMMERCIAL RADIO

In 1977, Mexico had 584 AM and 110 FM radio stations. Of these, only 17 AM and 5 FM stations were in the non-commercial sector. It is therefore commercial competition which heavily influences the station location and coverage.

Four-hundred-and-one AM stations - 71 per cent of the total - are concentrated in 12 of the nation's 32 states. These states are in the north and centre, precisely those areas which are more affluent. The FM stations follow the same pattern. Forty-four of the existing 110 stations are concentrated in the 3 most developed states. There are also 15 short-wave stations in Mexico, 9 of which are located in the capital.

The ownership of commercial radio is not as concentrated as television ownership. The medium does not require the heavy initial capital that television does, and radio stations can be run without incurring the large expenditures characteristic of television. The differences have made possible the creation of numerous independent stations. Nevertheless, the majority of stations are affiliated to or incorporated into national organisations to facilitate commercial exploitation. In 1977 15 networks contained 84 per cent of commercial stations.

Networks make administration cheaper, and enable broadcasters to exchange soap-operas and other fairly elaborate programmes which, in turn, can be produced by a professional, specialised, central creative organisation. The government favours this tendency to centralisation since, from their point of view, it facilitates regulation and control.

Given the large number of radio stations in Mexico, it is not feasible to analyse the organisational structure of individual companies. However, most of the stations share similar profiles and employ common components. In its simplest form, the small station's organisational chart will show a director general or general manager over a second echelon composed of executives handling marketing and sales, administration and finance, and engineering and production (operations). Larger, more complex organisations have departments exclusively concerned with programming, news, production, and public relations. Most commercial radio stations are vertically organised with a well-defined chain of command, although a few organisations still favour a centralised system where all lines of authority converge on one executive (usually the general manager).

The small size and private character of most commercial radio companies makes it difficult to obtain reliable data on revenues and financing. But since all commercial operations generate their income from the sale of time, information on the advertising market may offer a good substitute. It is estimated that Mexico's total advertising revenues in 1976 amounted to $310 million (0.49 per cent of the GNP), an increase of 12 per cent over the previous year. Fifteen per cent of this sum was invested in radio.

Infrastructure

Most of the 567 commercial broadcasters have only low-powered transmitters and are limited to local coverage. Eighty per cent of the stations operate on 1 kw or less. The remaining 20 per cent have transmitters from 5 to 250 kw. Although on average there are 18 stations per state, this figure is deceptive due to the already noted uneven distribution of facilities. There are some states with 40 stations and one state, in the south, with only two.

Radio sets are relatively inexpensive in Mexico. Transistors and portable power sources make it possible for rural areas to enjoy radio without requiring sophisticated electric power. Consequently radio has consistently expanded its coverage and number of listeners. Figures for 1977 show 7,456,986 radio homes with an estimated audience of 44,741,916, or 75 per cent of the total population. Territorial coverage is 100 per cent.

Because capital outlay needed for radio production is

in no way comparable to the vast amounts needed for television broadcasting, most radio stations have the means to originate some form of programming. However, more and more stations are using NAB cartridge systems for 'automated' broadcasting. Central rather than the local production of soap-operas and comedy programmes is becoming the rule, with production organisations located in large cities like Mexico City, Monterrey and Guadalajara. Consonant with these trends, a growing number of operators are becoming convinced that typical 'network broadcasting patterns' are no longer profitable. Many are converting their repeaters into local stations.

The centralisation of radio production facilities can be indirectly detected by examining the structure of Mexico's record industry. There are 52 record companies in the country, 90 per cent of which have their production studios in the capital city. Of the 15 principal record companies enjoying 89 per cent of the total market, nine are Mexican and six transnational. However, 57 per cent of the market belongs to the top 5 companies, 4 of which are multinational corporations. This situation matches the wide diffusion of foreign music on commercial stations. On the other hand, it has also resulted in the export of Mexican music.

In 1971 there were 15,000 persons employed by the radio and television industries. Until the early 1960s a serious problem in the radio industry was the shortage of qualified employees at all levels. However, today, technical schools and the universities are preparing personnel in a variety of categories including engineering and general communications studies, and more than 50 schools offer communications curricula. Graduates, however, are more attracted to the 'glamorous' media like television and film or to advertising agencies, than to radio. Four principal unions serve the majority of radio employees and 5 associations cover the industry's different professional facets.

Output

In the 1940s and 1950s radio employed a formula of music-news-comedy-drama-sports plus advertisements. Gradually a simpler pattern emerged. It emphasised music and advertising with short newscasts or hourly bulletins coupled with 'newsbreaks', 'updates' and 'flashes'. The popularity of television has led to this formula being modified in the direction of more specialised programming, and now the broad spectrum formats are being replaced by more narrowly focused programmes aimed at selected target audiences.

Stations adopt a 'personality' and are recognised because they spotlight news, live sport, soap-operas or some specific style of music. In Mexico City one station limits itself to broadcasting the exact time minute-by-minute with commercial spots sandwiched in between.

A study of the 32 stations covering the Mexico City metropolitan area, carried out in 1976, revealed that 69 per cent of total transmission time was devoted to 'light entertainment' (popular music, sports, comedy, drama and soap-opera). Twenty-five per cent of the remaining time was used for advertising messages. Only 6 per cent featured news, current affairs or special services.

An investigation in 1974 into the musical preferences of the Mexican radio audience indicated that Mexican songs were more popular than foreign ones. A sample of 180 popular songs as listed in the industry's music charts and stations' 'hit parades' showed that 65 per cent were Mexican. The remaining 35 per cent was made up of 15 per cent Spanish and Latin American tunes, 14 per cent North American titles and 6 per cent various European.

In spite of the fact that approximately only 6 per cent of Mexico City's daily schedules is given over to news, recent years have shown a marked improvement in the quality of broadcast journalism. Specialised news departments are an important part of large radio organisations like Nucleo Radio Mil, Organización Radio Centro, Organización Radio Fórmula and Sistema Radiopolis. The latter underlines its news orientation by having one station, XEX, function as a 'radio journal' with programming exclusively composed of news and advertising.

On the other hand, news services frequently suffer severe handicaps. Many broadcasters (Radio Centro is one) insist that news must be 'self-financing' through the sale of advertising time. In this concept news is not a 'service' but is regarded as a form of 'entertainment' which must generate its own specific time sales.

Although there are no available detailed figures analysing national newscasts, the above-mentioned 1976 study of 32 Mexico City stations does give us some insight into the make-up of broadcast 'news'. These figures are based on the telexed information sent to affiliates by the main transmitter stations of the programmes relayed to provincial stations.

TABLE 2   Breakdown of news content on Mexico City stations

Topic	Percentage of transmission time
Political information	30.0
Sports	20.0
Economics	11.0
Official government bulletins	11.0
Social items	9.0
Cultural material	8.0
Crime	3.0
Various	8.0

Of the total material used by newscasters, there is a clear preponderance of foreign information sources and stories. The big radio organisations are largely dependent on the international press agencies: UPI, AP, AFP, Latin Reuters, EFE, and others. Local press bureaux include Informex and Notimex, a quasi-state enterprise. The use of foreign press groups with comparatively vast news-gathering resources does account, to some extent, for the preponderance of non-Mexican items on the average news programme. But it should be noted that an editorial prejudice in favour of foreign news also exists and contributes to the elbowing of local information off the air.

There is no formal censorship. Mexican broadcast journalism operates on a basis of voluntary editorial control. There is no official review of material prior to broadcast. Each radio organisation establishes its own guidelines and follows them as internal editorial policies. The provisions laid down in the Ley Federal de Radio y Televisión enter into the formulation of such a policy. The Law declares the right of the public to objective information; prohibits the invasion of privacy; proscribes news that might endanger or threaten national security; sets up standards of language, and so on.

Commentary and current affairs programmes have never found much favour with Mexican broadcasters. Some material of this kind is produced by the Government through the Dirección General de Radio, Televisión y Cinematografía. Other programmes falling into this category are obtained from (among other sources) the BBC, Voice of America, Radio Netherlands. According to article 65 of the Ley Federal de Radio y Televisión, all foreign commentary and current affairs programmes must be submitted to the Ministry of the Interior for authorisation before being broadcast.

Above and beyond the high percentage of political information in the news (30 per cent), the government, as mentioned in Chapter 3, reserves the right to 12.5 per cent of the total transmission time of all stations. This time is intended to be used for public service and information material supplied by the government. Programmes have included the Presidential State of the Union Message and several Congressional inquiries. For many years the one such government show, *La Hora Nacional* ('The National Hour'), has been broadcast on a nationwide network, pre-empted for the purpose, every Sunday evening. A change in policy is forecast which would make it compulsory to broadcast 'The National Hour' but not necessarily by all channels in the same time slot.

Local stations in rural areas have developed several kinds of social service that make them unique. Some stations carry messages to isolated or remote individuals (for which a nominal fee is charged). In urban centres stations will help locate missing persons, and customarily provide time for social-service spots and announcements by non-profit-making organisations.

Research

Research in commercial radio is predominantly quantitative, not qualitative, particularly in the area of audience research. Various companies (eg, INRA, ANAM and Noble) provide radio stations with ratings. INRA (International Research Associates), the largest audience research agency, carries out 16,000 monthly interviews to obtain coincidental and recall data.

Mexico City is obviously the best served area for this kind of research. It now receives montly reports on audience fluctuation. The provinces are measured only twice a year as the cost of 'rural' studies is so much higher. In a typical audience analysis the socio-economic strata is taken into account (Class AB - upper, Class C - medium, Class D - low) as well as geographical location and time period.

Chapter 4

Public relations

The concept of public relations departments, both in radio and television, has not taken firm roots as yet.

Public relations are handled by the various professional guilds and associations, such as the Cámera Nacional de la Industria de Radio y Televisión, which attempt to foster a positive public image, promote cooperation among members and engage in some lobbying of the government. With the exception of only the largest enterprises, however, consistent public relations programmes are unheard of. The functions normally conducted by professional public relations personnel are usually handled on an 'intuitive' basis by department heads who have this responsibility added to other duties. Most of this effort is pragmatic, and largely influenced by letters and phone calls from the public expressing personal likes and dislikes.

In its infancy, like television, radio was seen as a threat to the printed media. But, once radio was firmly established and after sponsors had made their decisions regarding their allocation of advertising budgets, newspapers and magazines seemed to relax their hostility and found it convenient to carry weekly programming of radio stations as well as news about radio personalities.

Since many of the pioneer entrepreneurs in the industry came from publishing backgrounds, there was never any truly open confrontation between the media.

2 CULTURAL AND EDUCATIONAL RADIO

In contrast to the commercial radio, the cultural and educational radio stations have remained fragmented and restricted. There are now only 33 stations, 17 of which are AM, 5 are FM and 11 are shortwave. Unlike some other developing countries, Mexico has not carried out a systematic approach to the use of radio for educational purposes. Only a few isolated projects have been carried out.

The country's unequal socio-economic regional distribution affects the geographical location of cultural and educational radio stations as it does commercial stations. Out of the 33 stations, 30 are concentrated in the northern and central states. Mexico City alone has 8 stations.

44 Chapter 4

Since in the past the state by tradition has been charged with the responsibility to provide education and to raise cultural levels, the government has played the major role in the development of cultural and educational radio. It now owns 24 stations including 18 stations run by state universities and technical institutes. The remaining 9 belong to private non-profit-making organisations.

All the cultural stations are financed through subsidies, while educational stations are financed through donations from trustees, social welfare organisations and international funding agencies.

There are 17 university stations in the republic: 9 AM, 2 FM and 6 shortwave. Radio Universidad of Mexico City, a non-commercial station, belongs to the Universidad Nacional Autónoma de México (Autonomous National University of Mexico). Operating on an entirely autonomous basis, without government intervention, the UNAM's Radio Universidad is integrated into the Department of Cultural Dissemination of the University which finances its operations.

The objective of this station, as of the other university stations in the country, is to provide cultural and educational programmes at university and other specific educational levels. Eighteen hours are transmitted daily. The schedules include classical music, talks and discussions on history, the economy, social sciences, literature, theatre, painting, poetry and other arts, and critical commentaries on current publications. An 'international' section as well as a 'children's' section have been developed.

Radio Universidad has 5 news programmes, 4 of which are broadcast daily while the fifth consists of a weekly analysis in depth. The station relies on Informex for most news though some is supplied by its own reporters. With three recording studios, the station has a staff of 80, all of whom belong to the university employees' union, STUNAM. The UNAM's radio station maintains close contact with the other university stations of the country, exchanging programmes and offering them advice and support.

After being closed down in 1946, Radio Educación was re-opened in 1969 under the supervision of the Ministry of Public Education and the administration of the Dirección General de Educación Audiovisual. The station, with a

Chapter 4

staff of 120, has 5 departments and a public relations section and a director general. The departments are: production, administration, research, continuity, management and policy.

Radio Educación has 2 studios and broadcasts 19 hours a day, except at weekends when its output diminishes slightly. Programming basically consists of music, both national and international, with a special emphasis on folk music. It also broadcasts classical music combined with features, and news spots of a cultural character focused on literature, cinema, the plastic arts, music, science and education. Educational programmes, such as English-language lessons, along with discussions of art and entertainment, are also popular.

Three news bulletins are broadcast daily. The principal transmission takes place in the evening when Radio Educación links up with the cultural television station, Channel 11. The material for the other bulletins is drawn from the newspapers and provided by the station's own reporting staff (to date, no news agency services have been contracted). Information on activities carried out in the universities of Mexico City is also included, along with a cultural 'calendar' of current events.

In San Luis Potosi, a state to the north-west of Mexico City, a pilot project was initiated in August 1969 under the title of Radioprimaria. It is an attempt by the Dirección General de Educación Audiovisual y Divulgación (DGEAD) of the Ministry of Public Education to bring primary-level schooling to rural areas. Radioprimaria was also established in the state of Veracruz, where there are two transmitters; one in Huayacocotal, the other in Poza Rica.

According to a brochure of the Ministry of Public Education one of the principal aims of the project is to enable children in rural communities, who attend schools of less than 6 grades, to complete primary education in the conventional 6-year period. The basic idea behind Radioprimaria is to make up for the lack of funds to hire an adequate number of teachers at the primary level. By using radio the existing teachers can reach more children.

Broadcasts began in the 1970-1 academic year using the Ministry of Public Education's official curriculum for the fourth, fifth and sixth grades (the only grades served by Radioprimaria). According to 1976-7 figures, the course reached 2,700 pupils between the ages of nine and twelve. The programming material is prepared and recorded by a team of 14 teachers in Mexico City, in the two DGEAD studios. The tapes are then delivered to Veracruz and San Luis Potosí along with the Correo Radioprimaria (Radioprimary Post). As mentioned above Veracruz has its own transmitters while in San Luis Potosí the tapes are aired by the university station, XEXQ, free of charge, throughout the week.

In a 5-hour school day, radio lessons take up approximately 1 hour and 30 minutes. No lesson lasts more than 15 minutes. The primary course concentrates on Spanish, arithmetic, social sciences, nature study and practical activities. After the broadcast, the local teacher extends the teaching session with work projects initiated by the radio teacher. This is facilitated by the use of free textbooks provided by the Ministry of Public Education. The supervision of schools operating in the Radioprimaria system is carried out by zone inspectors who advise and encourage teachers. The Correo Radioprimaria guidelines sent to all teachers concerned contain a breakdown of radio classes as well as instructions covering activities for students before, during and after the broadcast.

In an evaluation of the Radioprimaria system certain factors must be taken into account. Problems to do with administration and hardware problems have sometimes distorted or aborted the goals of the system. Radioprimaria needs additional funding from the Ministry of Public Education if it is to develop. Results, to date, do not meet the objectives laid out by the Ministry itself. For example, in a total of 70 incomplete primary schools in San Luis Potosí, only 7 have been raised to sixth-grade level, while 36 of the 44 radio schools in the state were already teaching the full primary course before Radioprimaria began.

An interesting radio school experiment, run by Jesuits, has been carried out in the north of Mexico, in the state of Chihuahua, involving 46 schools in 9 municipalities of the Tarahumara region. Unlike the Radioprimaria experiments, the Tarahumara radio schools offer only the first 4 primary grades. The teaching is in Spanish even though most of the indigenous Tarahumara population speak only their own Indian language. It is estimated that in 1971 the Tarahumara radio schools reached 1,081 pupils.

As well as the radio teachers, each school has 1 or 2 auxiliary teachers who have completed the sixth grade of primary school. Their function is to follow the instructions of the radio lessons and to supervise the students. These lessons are within the established norms of the official curriculum for the primary course and are supplemented by free textbooks distributed by the Ministry of Public Education. When the programmes are broadcast to a specific grade, the other students in the same classroom are expected to continue with their own work.

In operation since 1965, Radio Tarahumara is a private venture. It is financed by 3 committees who are responsible for obtaining institutional and individual donations. However, these gifts are not enough to cover costs and therefore long-term planning is almost impossible. Shortage of money has also caused a serious problem. Many teachers either abandon the schools or are obliged to take on outside work.

In 1971 an evaluation of the Tarahumara system found that funding problems had hindered the continuous operation of the radio schools and therefore the goals had not been met. Another factor seriously affecting the system was the high drop-out rate caused by the pressure on many pupils to contribute toward family income.

The Departamento Radiofónico Bilingue (Bilingual Radio Department) of the Ministry of Public Education was created in 1972 to use radio to teach Spanish to indigenous communities. The department, with an annual budget of one million pesos, is divided into three sections: engineering, education and administration. Programmes are designed for primary school children and have been developed in different Indian tongues, chiefly those spoken in the southern and central regions of Mexico. However, due to a lack of funds, only the Otomí programmes have so far reached the air. These have been broadcast to 65 communities in the Valle del Mezquital in central Mexico. Working material is provided jointly by primary school teachers and trained mass communications technicians. Two indigenous teachers are included in each ethnic project group.

The didactic material consists of recordings, drawings and programme guidelines. Classes are conducted by teachers in conjunction with the recordings. In many cases indigenous instructors known as 'cultural promoters' teach the class. In order to qualify as a 'promoter' in a specified region, the teacher must be absolutely bilingual and have completed primary school. Classes are transmitted from Monday to Friday with a maximum duration of 20 minutes per class. Currently, the Bilingual Radio Department has 1,400 programmes available.

3 ADDITIONAL RADIO AND AUDIO-VISUAL EDUCATIONAL CAMPAIGNS

In the late 1960s, radio and television combined to carry out a literacy campaign on a national level. The project was devised and developed by the Consejo Nacional de la Publicidad (National Advertising Council), whose initial goal was to reach the illiterate population with news of the imminent inauguration of literacy courses by radio and television.

The courses themselves began in 1970 and those enrolled were entitled to receive a book, 'Yo Puedo Hacerlo' (I Can Do It'), and an accompanying exercise book. The published material was distributed by participating stations and schools. The transmissions were nationwide. Radio and television schedules were staggered for public convenience. In order to make these broadcasts possible, and to cover the greatest possible geographic area, the government made use of the 12.5 per cent broadcasting time allotted to it by the federal law regulating television and radio.

Evaluations of the campaign were unfortunately rather limited. But public education authorities feel that approximately 1 per cent of the illiterate population of Mexico learned some skills in reading and writing. This figure was arrived at partly by analysing correspondence written by students in examinations or in search of further information. Many participants wrote to express their gratitude or to seek access to more advanced teaching. Judging by the volume of mail received, it was estimated that more than 50,000 persons began the courses.

Yo Puedo Hacerlo was followed by a second course, 'Un Poco Más' ('A Little More'), whose objective was to teach or complete primary classes. Students who had enrolled in the first course were awarded credits and given grades which permitted them to move on to the next level. The agency in charge of these classes and their participants was the Departamento de Alfabetización (Department of Literacy) which, until 1971, functioned under the supervision of the Dirección General de Educación Audiovisual.

Chapter 5

COMMERCIAL AND NON-COMMERCIAL TELEVISION

At the beginning of 1972 there were 79 television stations in Mexico, all but one of which were commercial. The business was, like the radio business, highly competitive for its audience, and this dictated key factors like location, demographic coverage and the message orientation of the business organisations holding the franchises.

Most of the stations were concentrated in the main urban centres of those northern and central states which constituted markets strong enough to make the stations economically viable. Relatively sparsely-populated regions, and low-income areas, had marginal or no television services.

In May 1972 the government officially recognised the inequities of this situation. It established Televisión Rural de México (TRM), a television network specifically devised to supplement commercial systems in the grossly under-serviced rural regions. TRM did not attempt to compete with existing systems. It chose its service areas and focused its programming with the aim of reaching territories and audiences hitherto neglected.

The spread of TRM meant that by 1977 the numerical imbalance was somewhat redressed. There were now 119 stations in the commercial sector and 124 in the non-commercial sector (121 of which belonged to TRM), making a total of 243 on-the-air stations.

The adjustment was, however, more apparent than real since the commercial sector still commanded marked advantages in the areas and population covered. It also enjoyed considerably superior production facilities and employed more experienced professionals.

The financing of Mexican commercial television follows the established pattern now common on the American continent. Ownership is generally concentrated in the hands of those who have enough economic resources to capitalise and operate these enormously costly systems. Nevertheless, the structure of ownership of Mexican television does have one important novelty. The state itself participates in the industry as a proprietor or entrepreneur in the commercial sector. This has been true since 1972 when the government acquired Mexico City's Channel 13.

Once it had become a quasi-state project, Channel 13 expanded economically and technically. By 1977 it was the nucleus of a national network of 28 repeater stations covering a great part of the republic. The presence of Channel 13 has, indeed, acted as a healthy stimulus to competition for sponsors and audiences.

In 1972 the major networks of Telesistema Mexicano (TSM) and Televisión Independiente de México (TIM) were well established and able to meet the new challenge to their markets. By 1977, TSM was operating with 3 channels in Mexico City and 12 repeater stations. The creation of Televisa, SA, as a joint-venture company, in which TSM and TIM pooled facilities and coordinated programming, gave the new organisation a unique opportunity to carry out fiscal reforms in favour of commercial stability and thoughtfully to accept the broadcasters' civic responsibility.

This interaction of forces has served to bring into being a television industry that is peculiarly Mexican and which shows signs of an ability to change and grow within a singularly appropriate framework. The emerging paradigm will almost certainly lead to fresh forms, which should be especially sensitive to public needs as opposed to the demands of commerce and competition.

To fill in the picture of the commercial sector it is necessary to examine the pattern of operations in the 'provinces' where there are 14 channels with varying capacities for originating their own programmes. Ownership is dispersed among local investors. However, all of these independent channels affiliate with TSM and, part of the time, act as repeaters for the Mexico channels.

The primarily 'communications' orientation of commercial television goes beyond a solely 'video' point of view. Since the original owners of TSM, for instance, were already involved in communications media (including radio, publishing and film production) a whole range of media attitudes and ideas have persisted and influenced policy. Collateral interests of this kind immerse Televisa in a more or less complete 'communications environment'.

Advertising is a crucial factor in this environment. It is estimated that 50 per cent of Mexico's total advertising revenue (US $310 million in 1976) went to television. Televisa received 93 per cent of the total while Channel 13 and the remaining independent television stations shared 7 per cent.

Televisa is totally financed by the sale of advertising time. Channel 13, on the other hand, receives a government subsidy. An attempt is being made to free Channel 13 from dependence on state financing. The station's signal has now been vastly improved. Programming is constantly being upgraded. A more open policy toward the acceptance of advertising has been adopted and advertisements promoting alcoholic beverages and cigarettes are no longer so taboo.

1   TECHNICAL DEVELOPMENT

In the technical development of television in Mexico, the impact of the XIX Olympic Games in 1968 was profound. A broadband microwave network was created between the United States border and Mexico and the government installed a satellite ground station in Tulancingo. The microwave network, in its first stage, included 21 trunk routes running from Mexico City to the northern border. The system could carry multiple television and television and telephone signals for a total of 11,942 kms uniting the Telecommunications Control Tower in Mexico City with the Texas border.

The original network was built and operated by a private company, Teléfonos de Mexico, SA. After the games, the system was acquired by the government and then operated and expanded by the Ministry of Communications and Transport (SCT) through the Dirección General de Telecomunicaciones (DGT). By 1977 the Red Federal de Microondas (Federal Microwave Network) had under development 43,958 km of RF channel. The commercial stations used 18,881 km while the educational and cultural stations had 32,126 km.

The development of a microwave capacity had profound consequences on Mexican communications. Telecommunication between the United States and Mexico was substantially improved and made less costly. But the most important result was that television was able to achieve almost blanket coverage of the entire republic.

An ancillary development was the establishment and growth of cable television systems in Mexico City and other urban centres. By 1977 there were 46 operating CATV systems serving 65 urban centres and a further 31 systems in various stages of installation. The systems pick up their signals in Mexico City and re-transmit them through the Red Federal de Microondas. The signals are then reprocessed and delivered to subscribers in various fringe reception areas.

There are no official statistics on the total number of television sets in the republic. Many sets come in through irregular and illegal channels and do not appear in the Department of Commerce's figures. However, in 1977, the number of television homes reached by Televisa was reliably estimated at 5,223,495. The figures for 1971 were 2.5 million, 3.3 million for 1974 and for 1975 4.0 million. By multiplying the total number of television homes by five (the estimated average number of persons in a television home), Televisa has a 1977 estimate of 28,117,475 potential viewers. Channel 13, with 3,608,390 homes, would have 18,041,950 viewers. Thus it seems that Mexican television has technically achieved a 70 per cent coverage of the national territory but only reaches 43 per cent of the total population. This peculiar imbalance of demographic statistics in comparison with TV coverage is characteristic of many under-developed nations and it is true for most of Latin America. In other words, Mexican technical prowess has outstripped the level of standard-of-living and consequently it is now economic factors that restrict receiver ownership to 43 per cent of the population.

No reliable breakdowns of rural and urban audiences exist. Still, given the primarily urban orientation of commercial television, the high cost of a television receiver to the consumer (sometimes greater than a farmer's income) and the relatively poor supply of electricity in the rural areas, it can be assumed that the great majority of the farm population does not have television. This is further corroborated by the fact that 37 per cent of Televisa's audience is concentrated in Mexico City while 55

Chapter 5

per cent of Channel 13's total number of viewers is massed in the same area.

Attempts have been made to extend television coverage to rural regions. TRM claims 15,000,000 viewers. They cannot, however, give any reliable estimate of how this number is broken down into rural and urban audiences. Until the cost of receivers comes down, until rural electrification becomes more widespread, and until more effective means are found to reach farm families, viewing will be heavily weighted in favour of city dwellers.

The magnitude of the difficulty can be appreciated by examining the penetration of electric power. According to figures published in July 1977 by the Comisión Federal de Electricided, the quasi-state enterprise that controls Mexico's electric system, only 51 per cent of the total population has access to sophisticated electricity supply.

2 TELEVISA

In addition to its contribution to the development of Mexican television, Televisa had assumed by 1977 the role of a full-blown communications conglomerate consisting of 45 participating companies. These companies operate chiefly in the areas of television, radio and publishing. The advent of Televisa in this new role has involved new attitudes in management and a new awareness of the responsibility to the public that lies inherent in the functioning of this type of communications apparatus.

A key factor in Televisa's corporate organisation is the 'joint-venture' approach in which TSM and TIM remain in existence but lease to Televisa their respective transmitters, studios and equipment. Policy is the province of Televisa's Board of Governors; management lies in the hands of the companies' executives, whose main thrust is the elimination of inefficiency and waste on all levels. These changes made it possible to examine audience potential from the qualitative as well as the quantitative point of view which, in turn, meant a more sensitive appreciation of viewer's needs. To the sponsor this new policy paid dividends in lower production costs and in the offer of the most attractive package of saturation coverage ever put together in the history of Mexican television.

Interesting features of Televisa's organisations chart

(see Appendix) include the unification of production and engineering operations under one head; the separation in news programming of the journalistic function from the production function; the joint management of planning and development; and the joint administration of radio, television and magazine advertising. The advantage of most of these measures is self-evident, but it should be particularly noted that the focus on getting the news is sharpened, and the esprit that had been disappointingly absent from many television news departments has been considerably enhanced by the separation of functions.

Televisa's financing depends entirely on advertising revenues. A look at the advertising revenue for 1976 should help explain the corporation's operational pattern. Television brought in about $144 million, while radio totalled $4 million, CATV advertising revenues came to $960,000, magazines' $960,000. The corporation's total sales came to approximately US $184 million. In other words, television alone accounted for 78.26 per cent of Televisa's total revenues.

Advertising takes up 20 per cent of total programming time: in every hour, 12 minutes are used for commercials, call letters and channel logos. The minimum commercial spot is 20 seconds; 30- , 40- and 60-second spots are also available. Rates vary according to a cost-per-viewer formula combined with an evaluation of the time slot when the advertising message is to be aired. Time classifications are: Class A: 00.00-17.00 hrs; Class AA: 17.00 to 19.30 hrs and Class AAA: 19.30 to 24.00 hrs.

The consolidation of the sales departments of TSM and TIM did away with competition for advertising revenue and enabled clients to be served more expeditiously and with no distortion of their time needs. On the other hand, internal advertising and market research has suffered. Televisa has adopted an attitude that puts the burden of such investigation on the client. Unfortunately few Mexican companies operate on a scale large enough to justify this kind of special attention to sales analysis in reference to media and, obviously, some advertising money simply goes to waste.

Corporate re-organisation lumped television, radio and magazine time and space sales in one organisation which greatly facilitate the overall selling task. The department works closely with more than 90 of the 152 advertising agencies registered in the republic. The sales operational staff is 101.

TABLE 3 Televisa's networks

Channel	Area	Owner	No. of stations	Households
2	National	TSM	55	5,213,958
4	Mexico City	TSM	2	2,282,442
5	Regional	TSM/TIM	18	4,032,333
8	Valley of Mexico	TIM	3	2,200,212

Except for the 12 independent stations affiliated to TSM, Televisa's production facilities are concentrated in two installations in Mexico City. The 2 production centres, Chapultepec and San Angel, have 11 fully equipped studios, 42 colour cameras, 12 telecines, 21 VTRs, 1 slow-motion disc, 4 remote control units, 5 complete microwave channels and 4 emergency transmitters. Ancillary facilities include carpentry lofts, scenery docks, machine shops; prop, costuming and make-up departments; special effects departments and ample warehousing. Continually up-dating its hardware, Televisa spent almost $7 million on equipment in 1976.

That year also saw the beginning of a total reorganisation of Televisa in an attempt to modernise and systemise its operating and programming machinery. Top-level executives, aided by outside management experts, designed new methods and systems which were implemented in 1977.

An important innovation was the creation of a special department to coordinate the elements and facilities required to put together a programme. The intent was to free producers from repeated routine functions, making it possible for them to concentrate on creative tasks. Studio traffic, access to VTRs, audio recording facilities, scenery, etc., all came under this new department. The control of these many variables has already resulted in meaningful economies in time and money as well as in increased production values. Once material has been taped, the department delivers the tapes to Televisa's Continuity Department which, in turn, distributes the programmes to the Continuity Departments of the various channels.

Personnel statistics show that in 1977 Televisa employed 3,703 people, of whom 2,459 were on the monthly payroll. The remaining 1,244 were engaged through a regular but freelance arrangement. In addition, every month the various channels employ about 500 actors. Approximately 531 people are employed in administration, and 1,940 are technicians and creative staff. Thirty-seven per cent of Televisa's operational costs is for personnel and includes an annual bonus to each employee equivalent to two months' salary, social services, social security payments and other fringe benefits.

Each year Televisa transmits 21,423 hours of transmission, with each channel showing roughly 412 hours a week. of the total. Of this total, 60.9 per cent is locally originated and 39.1 per cent is imported (principally from the United States). In 1976, Televisa's programming costs reached about $32,400,000. Approximately $4,320,000 went to purchase imported material.

Through the elimination of inter-channel competition, Televisa feels that it has a chance to overcome some of the major drawbacks generally encountered in commercial television programming. Traditionally, literacy problems and low schooling levels force the medium to a species of no-holds-barred competition in order to obtain the lowest cost-per-thousand viewers for its advertisers. This invariably leads to a degradation in terms of programme content as greater and greater concessions are made to some assumed common denominator of taste.

The joint-venture approach has made it feasible to abandon this philosophy in favour of coordinate programming in which the four parallel channels serve audiences identified by means other than 'head counting'. The formula used for identifying the audience is essentially based on a theory of audience segmentation in which a certain number of channels operating together ensures that no significant social segment is ignored.

Channel 2's audience, for example, is made up of the rapidly expanding middle class and has an emphasis on soap-opera. Constant experiments are therefore made in the development of this kind of theatre with the object of giving it social and aesthetic significance. The remainder of the programming includes 'social service' broadcasts, children's programmes, sport coverage and evening comedy. Mexico's most prestigious news programme, '24 Hours', is aired during prime time.

Channel 4 serves the urban lower-middle class and

relies heavily on Mexican feature films. The backbone of its daily schedule is a four-hour magazine show which encourages both contact and feedback among the inhabitants of the capital city's many neighbourhoods (the concept of urban community). At weekends the emphasis shifts to sport.

Channel 5 appeals primarily to middle-class youth. American, British, Japanese and other filmed series are popular. Telesecundaria (Television Secondary School) is strip-programmed as a solid block during the morning hours.

Channel 8 aims at a higher cultural and educational level than the other channels. Artists of international reputation are featured and variety shows with excellent production values are not unusual. Internationally prestigious feature films (sub-titled) are a staple component.

The four Televisa channels attract the Mexico City audiences in this proportion: Channel 2, 44 per cent; Channel 4, 14 per cent; Channel 5, 25 per cent; and Channel 8, 11 per cent.

TABLE 4 Breakdown of Televisa's programming categories in a typical month (May 1977)

Category	Percentage of transmission time
Feature films	27.7
News	11.8
Social services	10.5
Children	10.3
Education	9.4
Filmed series	6.9
Drama	5.7
Culture	5.1
Sports	3.6
Musicals	2.7
Comedy	1.1
Game shows	0.5

By law, 12.5 per cent of Mexican air-time may be used by the government. Programmes in these slots are either cultural or political. Another factor in programme planning taken into account by Televisa when balancing its own schedules is the parallel activities of Channels 11 and

58   Chapter 5

13. Further, since the political reforms carried out in
early 1977, an effort has been made to provide access to
the air for new political parties and minority groups; in
1977 several special programmes gave representatives of
minority groups an opportunity to debate with leaders of
majority factions.

Televisa's annual news output totals approximately
2,847 broadcast hours. This is 13.3 per cent of the
network's total transmission time. Weekly production
(54 hours, 45 minutes) is distributed among 8 different
news programmes. Six of these show daily.

An analysis of Televisa's news programming (which is
applicable to television news in general) indicates that
television achieves a better balance between international and local material than does radio.

TABLE 5 Breakdown of Televisa's news content

Topic	Percentage of transmission time
Cultural material	50.9
Financial news	9.9
Sports	9.8
Social items	8.6
Political information	8.3
Official government bulletins	5.6
Crime	2.8
Various	4.1

Televisa's News Department has 250 employees and includes 56 national and 33 international correspondents.
The department uses Notimex and Informex for national
coverage. International news comes from AP, UPI, AFP,
Reuters and EFE with additional film material from SIN,
Visnews, CBS and NBC.

During 1976, total production costs, including staff,
came to about $5,360,000. This was 16.5 per cent of
Televisa's outlay for programming that year. Because
Televisa has a unified news department serving all channels, production costs average out notably lower than they
would if each station operated its own news-gathering
facilities.

Televisa engages in the world-wide sale and distribution of programme material. These functions are carried out by two autonomous corporations, Productora de Teleprogramas (ProTele) and Univisión. In 1976, ProTele exported 12,000 hours of videotape programming to Spanish-language stations all over the world. The bulk of these programmes was made up of *telenovelas* and comedy and variety shows.

ProTele also serves a national market and, during 1976, sold 5,000 hours to Televisión de Provincia and to various cable television systems. International sales reached $2,850,000 for the year, with national sales totalling 13 million pesos. ProTele also acts as producer for in-house commercials made by Televisa for clients.

A unique function of ProTele is the production of Video Reporte, a videocassette compilation of all television news broadcasts aired on the 6 channels of the capital. These cassettes are purchased by subscribers ranging from government ministries to academics and private individuals who want to 'monitor' Mexican broadcast journalism.

Univisión was created in the latter half of 1976 in order to serve the Spanish-speaking population of the United States. The programmes, originating in Mexico City, go to the border via the microwave system and are transmitted to 1,576,730 homes in eleven US cities by the domestic RCA satellite in conjunction with the Spanish International Network (SIN), a Televisa affiliate. By the middle of 1977 Univisión was broadcasting 19.5 hours per week, largely variety shows and sports. Emphasis is on Mexican folk and popular music. Boxing and soccer play an important role in sports coverage. The backbone of the schedule, however, is a news magazine show, *24 Horas* ('24 Hours') which runs nightly from Monday to Friday.

After forty years of suspended relations, Spain and Mexico renewed diplomatic exchanges in March 1977. Reaffirming Mexico's strong emotional and traditional ties with the Iberian peninsula, Televisa began operations in Madrid, cooperating with Radio Televisión Española (RTE). Broadcasts go through the Intelsat Atlantic satellite. The Madrid office also produces and co-produces 'specials' based on European talent.

From its beginning, Televisa has undertaken quantitative and qualitative audience research. Two coordinated departments provide input data to decision-making levels

of management. The Department of Information Services
specialises in processed quantitative data (audience
shares, etc.). Television ratings are based on 24,000
monthly interviews by INRA. Outside research organisations are occasionally contracted to provide additional
back-up services to the department. The other main
activity, qualitative research, is the province of the
Vice-Presidency of Research, recently created with a mandate to act as direct advisor to the President of Televisa. This research analyses the effects of different
formats and contents. An interdisciplinary approach is
used.

Actual operations are handled by the Instituto Mexicano
de Estudios de Comunicación (IMEC), the research arm of
the Vice-Presidency. IMEC departs from the usual studies
of audience fragmentation by shifting interest from socioeconomic criteria to 'communications codes'. The Mexican
television audience has been broken down according to
several codes which are under continuous study. The
department makes an effort to coordinate operations and
programming with observed data in regard to group preferences and requirements. As fresh facts accumulate, research findings are used to alter present practice or to
break new ground with innovative formats or content.
Televisa's dominant position in the industry allows it to
risk experiment more than a highly competitive situation
might permit.

Recent IMEC research, for example, resulted in the
planning, production and evaluation of *Ven Conmigo* ('Come
with Me'), a *telenovela* with the express purpose of supporting the Plan Nacional de Educación de Adultos (National Plan for Adult Education). The melodrama was engineered to motivate adults without primary education to
undertake studies offered in the 'open learning' system of
the Ministry of Public Education. The positive impact of
this experiment has influenced IMEC to schedule another
educational *telenovela*, this time to stimulate interest
and support for the government's extensive family-planning
campaign.

Initial plans outlining Televisa's corporate concept
included an integrated department to carry out internal
and external public relations. Today this group is made
up of 13 staff members and includes professional PR advisers and university-trained communications personnel.
The Public Relations Department advises and coordinates
management and the various divisions of the company. The

special spheres of interest represented by Televisa's semi-autonomous departments are thus projected effectively within the corporate framework without conflicting with goals established at higher levels. This applies to both internal personnel relations as well as to the solution of problems concerning the company vis-à-vis the public or government.

An attempt is made to deal with public relations by analysing and fragmenting the group to be reached. Typical groups are government officials, financial and banking community leaders, industrial sectors, academics, professional guilds and associations, etc. Viewers and advertisers (and potential advertisers), private citizen's interest groups are treated as separate categories. Also handled under the programme for external public relations are relations with foreign communications media as well as institutional relations with international associations.

Particular attention has been paid to developing close ties with the nation's academic community. Contacts with universities in Mexico and abroad are forged and relationships nurtured, particularly with those universities incorporating schools of communications. The chief aim of this effort is to encourage the formation of professionally qualified cadres for the nation's television industry.

Televisa cooperates with communications faculties by lending personnel to teach, by offering on-the-job training at Televisa and by a standing invitation to communications students to visit and study Televisa installations and methods. Joint research projects are funded and carried out and information is exchanged. Scholarships and leaves-of-absence enable Televisa's personnel to go on to post-graduate studies in engineering and communications in Mexico or abroad in the universities with which Televisa is in contact.

A mutually beneficial relationship has grown up between Televisa and the National University (UNAM), fostered by the intense effort required to put 'Introduction to the University' on the air. The production was developed and produced by Televisa's Cultural Foundation (FCT), while university faculty members provided the material used in scripting. A striking demonstration of the value of this kind of cooperation was seen during a recent strike of UNAM employees. In order to avoid any interruption of the series, and of the academic year, Televisa produced and transmitted 18 hours a day of 'classes'. Televisa's initiative was followed by Channels 13 and 11 as well as by 57 radio stations in the metropolitan area.

Letters and telephone calls provide the company's main contact with viewers and their organisations (mostly fan clubs). This kind of feedback is somewhat superficial but it does indicate the tastes and preferences of a certain segment of a station's public. The majority of the letters received are sent to 'TV-Guide', a Televisa affiliate. But because this type of information has limited value, Televisa is collaborating with the universities to promote the creation of various 'Tele-Clubs' whose purpose is the serious analysis of programming.

Televisa's relations with the publishing industry have by and large been good. Newspapers and magazines are the principal outlets for programming information and promotion. Press bulletins and photographs are provided on a regular basis. 'TV-Guide' publishes a television service and a fan magazine with a weekly 500,000 circulation. Televisa, in conjunction with a publishing house, also produces and markets 13 other periodicals, most of them directed toward mass circulation publics.

Televisa's Film Division purchases material for its four channels in both the national and international markets. A Cinema Division was organised in 1977 to make feature films. The company finances and produces not only its own features but also envisages more ambitious projects on an international scale, including co-productions with the United States, France, Italy and Spain. The company has already had some experience in this field and made some prize-winning films. A step in this direction, on a policy level, has already been taken. What used to be called a stable of stars is being groomed in an attempt to re-invigorate the local industry and to repeat the successes of the 'Golden' Era that lasted from 1930 to 1950. New 'star' talents are being encouraged, trained and contracted to television in the hope that their potential can be developed and put to use in feature films.

In order to maintain a pool of artists and to underwrite the careers of fresh talents, Televisa acts as impresario for many of the plays produced in Mexico City's lively theatres. Once the plays have finished their run, they may be televised and shown on one of the company's channels. This provides some financial security for writers, actors and directors.

Chapter 5

Televisa actively participates as a member of the Organización de la Televisión Iberoamericana (OTI) through which it has a working relationship with the television stations of all the Ibero-American countries and Brazil. Programmes and a daily news service are exchanged by Intelsat satellite through Servicio Internacional de Noticias (SIN), a part of OTI. Argentina, Brazil, Chile, Colombia, Mexico, Uruguay, Venezuela, Spain and Portugal are the participating members of SIN. All members have their own satellite stations except Uruguay which shares Argentina's facilities. In policy and operations SIN parallels the Eurovision news service. Its objectives are to increase the circulation and use of news from member countries in order to improve the understanding of culturally related nations, to eliminate the danger of projecting a purely Anglo-Saxon point of view of Latin America to the rest of the world, and to present a wide spectrum of material. The heart of the SIN operation is the Coordination Centre in Spain. The Chief Coordinator is chosen from a revolving roster of member countries, the post going to the representative of a different country every three months.

Every day at 13.00 hrs GMT a telephone conference via satellite is held with the full complement of coordinators. Each participant is given the opportunity to present his news 'budget'. Items which receive 3 votes are included in that day's news transmission. After this, SIN offers Eurovision the Ibero-American news in exchange for Eurovision's material. This material is recorded on videotape and then transmitted via satellite from Spain to participating countries at 19.10 hrs GMT. At the receiving end, the various member countries have the right to book a down-link if they wish to use the material. The only costs to the various organisations using SIN are a yearly fixed quota sum to contribute to the expenses of coordination, and a fee for each use of the optional downlink.

In the continuing effort to ensure freedom of expression and to define the relations of government and the mass media, Televisa belongs to the Asociación Interamericana de Radiodifusión, AIR (Interamerican Broadcasting Association). This group is particularly concerned with the legal aspects of the broadcast media. It is also an associate member of the European Broadcasting Union.

Televisa became an associated member of the United States National Academy of Television Arts and Sciences in

1975, at which time its organisation of the First Worldwide Communications Meeting was singled out for commendation. It is also a member of the United States National Association of Broadcasters and the International Institute of Communications.

In 1974, at a time when Televisa was becoming conscious of its growing role as leader in communications, a Worldwide Communications Meeting was organised and hosted by Televisa to bring together key figures in broadcasting, linguistics, sociology, entertainment and other communications-related fields. The objective was to encourage the exchange of information about communications. A second World-wide Communications Meeting was held in July 1979.

Televisa's Cultural Foundation (FCT) tries to serve the individual artist. Annual fellowships are given to artists to enable them to work without economic pressures. Four scholarships are awarded to youth leaders every year to enable them to participate in a seminar organised by the Hugh O'Brian Foundation of the United States. FCT also takes part in *Operación Plus Ultra*, a Spanish project meant to single out and reward youngsters who have shown outstanding humanitarian qualities. In Mexico, one child is chosen yearly to receive a 'complete' educational scholarship which takes him all the way up to and through university. Under FCT auspices, a programme to locate and recover pre-Columbian artifacts and archaeological pieces lost to Mexico through purchase and illegal traffic has been quite successful.

3 CHANNEL 13: THE CORPORACIÓN MEXICANA DE RADIO Y TELEVISIÓN

Channel 13 has been the backbone of the State's direct participation as a broadcaster and transmitter in the Mexican television system. Easily the most important government channel in the country, it is generally considered as an alternative or complement to the private television channels. In contrast to the majority of governmental broadcasting organisations in other countries, Channel 13 is markedly commercial. It was not always so. For many years the amount of advertising time was kept to a minimum. However, as the 1977 administrative reforms of the federal government took shape, subsidies made to quasi-state enterprises were decreased, and Channel 13 found itself obliged to become self-financing as far as possible through the sale of advertising time.

Chapter 5

The Administrative Council of Channel 13 is the policy-making body of the station. It is composed of representatives of the Ministries of the Interior, Public Education, Resources and Industrial Development and the Treasury, as well as representatives of Sociedad Mexicana de Crédito Industrial (SOMEX), a quasi-state credit institution which provides the Channel's financial backing. Top-level executives of Channel 13 are also members of the Council. As a consequence of the functional reforms and the need to increase the commercialisation of its programming, Channel 13 is undergoing a total reconstruction. At the time of writing, no relevant organisational chart is available.

From the $155 million spent on television in 1976, Channel 13 absorbed approximately $5 million, representing 3.23 per cent of the country's total advertising budget. This low percentage is easy to comprehend in the light of the Channel's policies relating to advertising from 1972 to 1976. With the revised policies, adopted in early 1977, advertisements for tobacco and liquor are now accepted and during the first half of 1977 Channel 13 almost tripled its revenues compared to the corresponding period of 1976. None the less, for some time to come, Channel 13 will continue to require a generous subsidy from SOMEX.

Channel 13's network is composed of 28 repeater stations widely distributed over the country, which provide nearly national coverage. These repeater stations serve 3,608,390 television homes or approximately 18 million viewers.

Originally Channel 13 was confined to the Mexico City metropolitan area, but in 1972, when the overnment took over, three stages of expansion were planned to blanket the country. The first stage was put into effect in 1974 and by 1977 the third stage was underway.

The master transmitter of the network, located in Mexico City, has an operating power of 312 kw, the maximum authorised for VHF broadcasting.

All the production facilities are also concentrated in Mexico City. The federal government invested heavily in 1976 in new installations, including 5 fully equipped studios, 24 colour cameras, 4 telecines, 8 VTRs, 1 slow-motion disc, 3 remote control units and 14 complete microwave channels. Channel 13 also has 2 rehearsal halls to help economise on studio time. Responsibility for all production facilities are centralised in one department, facilitating the producer's task.

Channel 13 has over 1,000 employees, including free-lancers. Sixty-two training courses were carried out in its first 4 years of operation under governmental control (mainly on-the-job teaching). Its annual output is 4,152 hours of which, in 1977, 56.2 per cent was of national origin and 43.8 per cent imported. Outside purchases are chiefly from European countries.

Although Channel 13 claims to be an alternative to private television, it seems to be still striving to define and locate its audience. Its current programming, however, is a somewhat incongruous mixture of 'elitist' material and material that attempts to appeal to the mass audience.

TABLE 6: Channel 13: breakdown of programme content during 1976

Topic	Percentage of transmission time
Feature films	22.09
Variety shows	13.58
News	9.47
Musicals	7.98
Serials	5.79
Public events	4.80
Drama	4.78
Science, arts, education and culture	4.43
Various	27.08

INRA reports that Channel 13's 1971 share of the Mexico City audience was 6 per cent, compared to 4 per cent in 1976. A possible explanation for these low figures is that Channel 13 lacks a well-defined programme policy that is easily recognised by viewers. A further reason could be that the Channel often interrupts its published programming schedule to transmit previously unadvertised programmes.

As Channel 13 is one of the most important outlets for government information, special emphasis has been placed on political broadcasting. According to the already mentioned multi-media study carried out in 1976, 46.3 per cent of Channel 13's news coverage was devoted to political information. Its official figures state that in 1976 it contributed 33.23 per cent of the total coverage of political events and 18.09 per cent of the total official messages transmitted on the entire Mexican television system.

Its annual news output, in 1976, was 392 hours, distributed between 2 major programmes, representing 9.47 per cent of the total. Channel 13's News Department works with Notimex and Informex for national news, while AP, AFP, Reuters, UPI and EFE provide international news. The station also participates in the information pool of Servicio Internacional de Noticias (SIN), a service offered by OTI. According to the multi-media study, 66.8 per cent of Channel 13's news coverage is national as against 33.2 per cent of international.

TABLE 7 Channel 13: breakdown of news content during 1976

Topic	Percentage of transmission time
Political information	46.3
Cultural material	14.8
Sports	12.6
Official government bulletins	10.0
Financial news	6.8
Social items	5.4
Crime	1.3
Various	2.8

Channel 13's audience research is predominantly quantitative. Qualitative studies are almost non-existent. A group of 15 interviewers of Channel 13 carry out approximately 250 daily interviews regarding television viewing and audience composition in the Mexico City metropolitan area. Viewers are divided, according to socio-economic strata, into Class A (medium-high), B (medium) and C (low). Other indicators are age, sex and education. There are also occasional interviews to obtain information on the Channel's coverage and its signal quality.

The Channel's limited budget does not allow for extensive public relations. The relations that do exist with other media (such as the press) are of a commercial character. The Public Relations Department is in charge of feeding the press with information about programming as

well as official bulletins. Relations with the public
and audience feedback are based on letters and telephone
calls as well as some public access programmes. Channel
13 is an active member of the Organizacion de la Television Iberoamericana (OTI) and an affiliated member of the
European Broadcasting Union. There is a continuing exchange of programmes with other countries (including Iran,
Bulgaria, Hungary, West Germany and Cuba). Channel 13
has also arranged for Mexican television material to be
shown in several cities in the United States.

4 NON-COMMERCIAL AND CULTURAL TELEVISION

Channel 11

Under the auspices of the Instituto Politécnico Nacional
(The National Polytechnical Institute) Channel 11 began
regular broadcasting in March 1959 as a non-profit-making
television station. Its beginnings were modest, with 40
employees working in production, operations and administration. But by 1977, the station needed 145 people to
operate a considerably expanded plant with a more demanding broadcast schedule.

Channel 11 has always been plagued by financial problems. Initiated on an austere budget by the IPN, the
available monies have had to be spread thin, and barely
covered basic needs. In 1974 the expenditure was given
to be approximately $1 million.

When Channel 11 started, Mexican television was ten
years old, but little attention had been paid to the educational and cultural aspects of the medium. In a pros-
pectus heralding its creation, the new station characterised itself as 'XEIPN, Channel 11, Latin America's first
cultural and educational station'. Goals were defined in
terms of 'informing' and 'teaching'.

After nine years of operation, a 1968 Presidential
Decree restructured the Channel. The Comision de Opera-
cion y Fomanto de Activadades Academicas (Commission for
the Promotion and Implementation of Academic Activities)
took over the station and converted it into a quasi-state
organisation. COFAA is headed by the Director of the
IPN. Financial matters are in the hands of the Treas-
urer, a post filled by the Director of the Bank of Mexico.
An Executive Secretary and four Commissioners named by the
Minister of Public Education complete the supervisory

board. In spite of its status as a quasi-state organisation directly under the federal executive, programming is not subject to government censorship or interference.

The station's management is obliged to report regularly to the Commission which acts as a policy and regulating agency. Its internal organisation includes an administration which is divided into a Department of Supervision, a Department of Production and a Department of Technical Guidance. At a lower level, there is a sub-directorate to which report the four managers responsible for administration, production and programming, for technical operations and interior/exterior public relations. Further subdivisions produce a rather complex managerial hierarchy.

The IPN's approach to programming has been consistent over the years. The heaviest emphasis is placed on content rather than form. An attempt is made to keep abreast of national cultural activities including theatre, dance, ballet, cinema and literature, history and the social sciences. Language teaching is prominently featured. Although the emphasis is on national activities, current international events are frequently covered. Channel 11 itself distinguishes between two kinds of programming: material which adheres to a conventional format and material which favours information and education. The first includes dramatic programmes, many of them 'avant garde' documentaries, and 'classic' films. In the second category the bulk of programming consists of talk shows, round tables, and presentations specifically designed to educate.

Channel 11 has three studios. For black-and-white work the station has a telecine, a mobile unit, 2 VTRs and a 20 kw transmitter. For colour, there is a mobile unit, 1 VTR, a film chain, and a 150 kw power plant.

According to its published figures, Channel 11 broadcast 2,600 hours in 1975. Of these, 1,456 were live, 832 were videotaped and 132 were films. The Channel is best known for 'live' programming - ballet, stage spectacles and concerts, and so on. Since 1977, it has broadcast 16 hours daily; 47 per cent is in colour. Its signal covers the Valley of Mexico, Pachuca and Cuernavaca.

Television Rural de México (TRM)

Television Rural de México (TRM) was created by Presidential Decree in 1972 to bring under-serviced rural areas into the national television system. Its general objective, as defined in its statutes, is to use television for national integration and to raise the cultural level of the population through the standardisation of spoken Spanish and through the cultural penetration of remote areas.

A government agency, called the Dirección General de Servicios de Television Rural de México, was attached to the Subsecretaria de Radiodifusion to implement this policy. The group was to be directly responsible for the expansion of TRM's services and for the establishment of local means to promote television viewing. The agency also had the task of maintaining the quality of the continuity and the services.

By 1977, TRM had 121 outlets of which 86 were operated via the microwave network while 35 were served by videocassette. The network reached a total of 15 million viewers. The control centre of TRM is located in Mexico City in the Telecommunications Control Tower where TRM also has a small studio with a camera, 2 VTRs and a film chain.

TRM's prime objective is to re-transmit television signals to areas which cannot pick up the regular signals. It has almost no production of its own, but draws on both commercial and governmental channels. Programmes are selected on the TRM Programming Council. Special emphasis is placed on the transmission of the organised audience ETV system called 'Telesecundaria'.

TABLE 8 TRM's transmissions during the second quarter of 1977

Programme supplier	Percentage of transmission time
'Telesecundaria' ETV system	24.00
Dirección General de Radio, Television y Cinematografia	17.10
Channel 13	16.00
Channel 11	9.00
Channel 8	7.60

Channel 5   12.00
Channel 4   5.80
Channel 2   3.00
TRM (station identifi-
cation)   5.50

The same decree that created TRM stipulated that the agency would have the right to choose any commercial television programme for transmissions providing that the programmes were broadcast in their entirety - that is to say, including advertisements. Thus, although TRM is a non-commercial, non-profit-making organisation subsidised by the government, it is, in practice, a mixed system.

Productora Nacional de Radio y Television

Until 1976, the Subsecretaria de Radiodifusion of the Ministry of Communications and Transport acted as a production agency for the government's 12.5 per cent of broadcasting time on the commercial stations, and for specific programming for the TRM network. Since mid-1977, following administrative reforms, these functions have been taken over by the Productora Nacional de Radio y Television (PNRT), a quasi-state company attached to the Ministry of the Interior, and equipped not only to fill the 12.5 per cent but also to commercialise its production services in order to become self-supporting.

Productora Nacional de Radio y Television is divided into three departments: radio, television and engineering. Its radio production facilities consist of 3 studios, each equipped with 2 tape recorders, 3 turntables and 2 cartridge systems. Television production facilities include three fully equipped studios, 10 colour cameras, 14 VTRs, 2 telecines, 3 remote-control units and 5 microwave channels. Since PNRT is still at a preliminary organisational stage, it provides only 3 per cent at present of the total 12.5 per cent of the programming time allotted to the government. Most of the slot is filled by programmes produced by the ex-Subsecretaria de Radiodifusion. However, it is hoped that before long this production agency will be fully operational and will produce all the programming required to fill the 12.5 per cent.

An account of the productions carried out by the ex-Subsecretaria de Radiodifusion from 1972 to 1976 will provide some insight into the use of the 12.5 per cent broadcasting time. Programmes during these years gave extensive coverage to Presidential activities, ministerial meetings, public enquiries and general information concerning national development. Programmes of a cultural nature were also produced, with particular emphasis on the country's history and customs as well as Mexican art, theatre and cinema. Some of these programmes were coproduced with European broadcasting organisations including ORTF, BBC, Telepool and others.

Dirección General de Educacion Audiovisual y Divulgación

The Dirección General de Educacion Audiovisual y Divulgación (DGEAD) was created in 1946 as a dependency of the Ministry of Education to produce, purchase, and distribute audio-visual educational material for radio and television. Its major field of action has been educational television, with the development of the Telesecundaria system designed to supplement the traditional school system as the Mexican government faces a growing school-age population and increasing demands for education at all levels. Telesecundaria provides a complete three-year secondary education for students who have no access to schooling beyond the sixth grade. The number of primary school graduates unable to enroll in secondary school in 1965 was more than 180,000, about 37 per cent of the previous year's sixth graders. This was particularly characteristic of rural areas where secondary schools are scarce, almost non-existent, and economically not feasible.

The Telesecundaria system was initiated in 1968 in seven central states of the republic as well as in the federal district. It complements rather than replaces the official secondary schools and the students are given the same status as students in the conventional school system. Although it follows the traditional curriculum, its resources are not only drawn from the Ministry of Public Education but also from local communities. Instead of federally-financed school buildings, the Telesecundaria classes take place in space supplied by the local communities which often form a parent organisation or *patronato* to provide the necessary hardware. Classroom coordinators are used to supervise instruction in place of fully accredited and specialised teachers. These coordinators are fifth and sixth grade teachers paid by the federal government. They undergo some special training in the use of television and are provided with monthly guidelines of the televised lessons. The DGEAD prepares student workbooks for the classes. These books are sold at a low cost in commercial bookstores.

Student enrolment for the academic year 1975-6 was 40,665, which represented an increase of 9.9 per cent over the previous year. Students receive 30 weekly televised lessons, each lasting 20 minutes. The remaining 40 minutes are devoted to preparation and follow-up activities under the coordinator's supervision. The tele-classes are produced at the DGEAD studios in Mexico City and are transmitted over Channel 5 which has donated over 40 per cent of its total transmission time to the Ministry of Public Education for use by the Telesecundaria system. The annual cost per student is calculated (1972) at $150. The annual cost per student in the traditional system is estimated at $200. However, it should be noted that an important component of these costs, that of transmission, is calculated on the basis of power, personnel, and maintenance only, as Televisa's Channel 5 absorbs the expenditure.

Fundacion Cultural Televisa

As the most influential communications organisation in Mexico, Televisa is aware of its social responsibility concerned with the developmental needs of the country, particularly in the field of education. In 1975, it created an autonomous cultural and educational non-profit-making foundation, Fundación Cultural Televisa (FCT), with the general purpose of 'raising the cultural levels of the Mexican population and supporting government efforts in this area'.

One of the priorities of the current government is to expand higher education in Mexico. A crisis in this area is imminent since the growth rate of the number of secondary school graduates is much greater than the potential growth rate of traditional higher education systems (universities and technological schools). With this in mind, the main target area of the FCT is in the field of higher education through the utilisation of open-circuit television. For this purpose, the FCT has concentrated on the planning and implementation of a university known as Universidad del Aire.

Universidad del Aire has been planned in three steps. The first is a preparatory stage called Introducción a la Universidad. Its objective is to provide students with vocational orientation and a solid educational background. It presents an intensive course meant to guide and attract new students to the universities and technological colleges. The second stage, Extensión Universitaria (University Expansion), involves the establishment of systematic courses to help the student complete his curriculum at the university level. The final stage is a conventional open university, somewhat on the model of the UK's Open University. The programme of professional courses follows the complete curriculum required for obtaining the equivalent of a Bachelor's Degree. The curricula offered will be determined by the educational demands deemed most in the national interest. It is hoped that the university will turn out professionals in several areas where skills are desperately lacking. The project was initiated just over a year ago and is still in the early stage of implementation. The 'Introducción a la Universidad' has been divided into four quarters and includes the History of Art, Anthropology, Zoology, Physics and Chemistry. Special emphasis is laid on making students aware of university and technical careers closely related to the real needs of the country. The object of these programmes is to introduce new interests and to avoid traditional professions where graduates can no longer be absorbed.

Academic support for the project is provided by a contract between the FCT and the Universidad Nacional Autónoma de México (UNAM), which specifies that the professors of the UNAM will supply the curricula on each subject along with the teaching material to be used in scripts written by FCT specialists.

The programmes are produced in Televisa's studios and transmitted on Channels 2 and 5 in the early afternoon. Transmissions started in January 1975 and a total of 1,130 hours were broadcast during that year. (If this broadcasting time had been used commercially, sales would have come to approximately US $6 million.) Production costs totalled $1,600,000.

In spite of the great hopes and considerable investment in 'Introducción a la Universidad', it has had an extremely low average rating during its first year on the air. Evaluations are being carried out to see whether these results are due to programming errors, faulty formats or to the fact that such material simply has a low audience appeal under any circumstances.

Chapter 6

THE FUTURE OF MEXICAN BROADCASTING

Over the years, both radio and television have undergone fundamental changes, not only in technology, but in basic conceptual terms. Initially both media were influenced by powerful commercial considerations and the electronic media were seen as entertainment and 'show business'. But the population explosion and ecological pressures have led to the growth of a different idea of social responsibility towards the use of the airwaves by both private enterprise and by the government. The mass media have become basic elements in the survival of civilisation.

In a series of interviews with government leaders and major figures in the Mexican communications industry a salient point emerged. There was universal concern about the enormous increase in population, which, according to responsible estimates, will grow from the current 62 million to reach 135 million in the year 2000. Of this number, 35 million will be concentrated in the metropolitan area of Mexico City. These staggering statistics underline the enormity of the problem of mass communications in Mexico's future.

Three areas of extreme sensitivity immediately suggest themselves. They are communication *qua* communication; public education; and cultural or national integration. Regardless of the political complexion of the interviewees, all agreed that the electronic media would play a vital role in the control of the potentially disruptive forces in these problem areas. The broadcaster must begin by asking the question 'who communicates what to whom?' In the interest of democracy and because of a strong desire to preserve freedom of expression, both government and industry leaders accept the fact that the possibilities of manipulating mass audiences and the extreme suggestibility inherent in the crowd mentality are ever-present threats to the continuation of political liberty. There is, however, no consensus as to how the access to communications channels and the safeguarding of free expression might be effected.

People in private enterprise seem to feel that one method to prevent flagrant abuse is the mixed system of alternative broadcasting, with both the private sector and the government participating. In the last decade the government has not been inclined to authorise new franchises or concessions. This attitude is, at present, restricting the growth of commercial television, both broadcast and by cable.

Both the government and private enterprise agree that there is little hope that conventional educational facilities can cope with the needs of the increasing population. One highly-placed executive at Televisa summed it up by saying that 'learning by sitting physically in a classroom will eventually become a rare privilege'. Formal education or direct teaching through the electronic media will, if predictions are correct, become the joint responsibility of both private enterprise and the government. In presenting 1977's new educational reforms, which provide for compulsory schooling up to the ninth grade, the Minister of Public Education emphasised the urgent need for the broadcasting industry and the state to work together to meet the educational goals of the nation.

Radio executives feel that their medium can fill a national need in a way that has, until now, been relatively unexploited. The Director General of Núcleo Radio Mil has pointed out that, within reasonable limits and taking into consideration the economic viability of the medium, it was a basic responsibility of radio broadcasters to provide instruction because only radio 'could achieve maximum access to all areas'. The President of Mexico, José López Portillo, affirmed the relevance of this statement when he said: 'the ability of radio to carry messages to marginal areas is a prime national resource'. The government's intention in regard to education is underlined in the recently announced Sistema Nacional de Comunicación Social (National System for Social Communication) which is being developed by the Dirección General de Radio, Televisión y Cinematografía. All sectors of the electronic media are participating in the preparation of this massive project, although at the moment there are no concrete operational plans. The government's original proposals are being re-appraised in depth by all elements of the industry before any definitive action is taken. There is a marked increase in cooperation between private enterprise and institutions of higher learning in the preparation and broadcast of informal educational material with the ultimate goal of transforming this type of semi-popular teaching into more formal direct education.

Recent successes in the use of ostensibly commercial formats in prime-time as conveyors of social and educational messages have elicited promises from executives in private enterprise that similar programmes will be tried in the future. The best results have been obtained through the use of melodrama with the story serving educational ends. This category of programming will be increased with the possibility of diminishing the present hold that soap-operas have over the early-evening Mexican viewer. Other experiments using game-show formats seem to indicate, particularly in radio, that the listener is willing to absorb a reasonable amount of educational material with his entertainment.

Although only a very slim line divides education from cultural programming, and cultural programming itself from attempts at national integration, statements as to the use of 'fiscal time' (the 12.5 per cent government time) would suggest that the majority of programme segments will be used to help specific audiences integrate into the national political system. Particular emphasis will be placed on providing the individual with a more complete knowledge of his rights and benefits under the various social welfare plans managed by the state. However, a strong influence on programme content in this area is the desire of the federal government to overcome localist tendencies towards decentralisation, and to forge what it considers a true Mexican nationality. This has been an historic problem due to the fragmented communications efforts and ethnic isolation caused by geographical divisions. Outside government circles, there exists some feeling that the loss of cultural pluralism might be a high price to pay for national unity.

It is a stated policy of the present government that it will make full use of its 12.5 per cent 'fiscal time' rather than expand government transmission facilities. This would indicate that the Mexican communications system will continue to develop with its facilities more or less in the same proportion as existed in 1977. An exception to this is the accelerated growth of the Television Rural de México network. The government feels that TRM is its responsibility since income is low and there is no feasible and economically viable way for private enterprise to participate on a free-market basis. While the overnment might reasonably take the attitude that reaching marginal areas was a duty inherent in the broadcasting franchise granted to private enterprise, current thinking indicates that such measures would violate the Mexican concept of a mixed economy in which private entrepreneurs are expected to operate for profit and without coercion. The importance of this policy becomes evident when demographic figures are projected into the near future, and it is estimated that 80 per cent of the nation's inhabitants will be located in or around cities. It is estimated that in 1980 the annual population growth rate will be 1.9 per cent in rural areas and 5.2 per cent in urban areas.

Even in government circles, production executives spoke strongly against giving the state total production responsibilities for those programmes scheduled to be aired on 'fiscal time'. Suggestions have been made that the 'fiscal' programming should be carried out by private enterprise as well as by the government in order to prevent the development of a monolithic structure which might lead to a lessening of both the quality and impact in programme execution and content.

There is some criticism of the imaginative element in local television. One prominent manager-producer puts it this way: 'television has always been focused on politics and economics rather than on creativity'; another top executive with production experience has stated that Mexican television unfortunately has never grown beyond being 'radio with a screen'. Allowing for the emotional overemphasis that comes from self-criticism, it is true that Mexican television has offered many well-made productions but very few programmes marked by real inventive novelty or exceptional talent.

However, the increasing number of communications schools that have creative instruction included in their curricula, and the fact that private enterprise is both encouraging and favouring professionally trained novices, would indicate that there may be a growth of originality in programming.

The following three facts stand out from the data gathered from the interviews. Communication via the electronic media will not be governed by solely commercial cri-

teria; coverage will be extended to reach a maximum
public through technical improvements and the lowering of
the cost-per-unit of receivers; and governmental regulation and participation in the communications industry will
be more centralised but will not include the physical expansion of quasi-state enterprises.

There has been a long-running controversy in Mexico as
to whether a microwave system or a domestic satellite
would be preferable for future telecommunication needs.
The balance of opinion in the industry seems to favour the
launching of a domestic satellite which, it is felt, would
provide wider national coverage as well as the possibility
of some kind of Inter-American Spanish-language network.
Current evidence suggests that such a satellite will be in
use within two years and that one of its immediate effects
will be to lower the cost of telecommunications within the
republic. This project is in a very early stage of development and there is no information on the type of satellite system to be adopted. At the present time it is
planned to use the satellite for government and commercial
television and for telephone communication.

The spread of cable television in Mexico is a particularly interesting indication of the movement within conventional television toward assuming a real role as an
instrument of mass communication. Reception by cable is
considered a luxury, but the demand in the major cities
has always exceeded capacity. In areas where cable alone
could solve problems of transmission, costs have never
proved to be a hindrance to its use or purchase by subscribers. Public attitudes toward cable television are
in some way 'elitist' but indicate a market for a special
kind and quality of commodity which may become rarer in
the future as population growth exerts its peculiar socioeconomic effects and some levels of programming disappear.
Unfortunately the Mexican government has followed a restrictive policy in the granting of cable concessions.
This reluctance is effectively slowing the growth of more
widely integrated systems. Although there is no stated
policy regarding the restrictive measures on cable television, the reasons for limiting franchises can be conjectured. One of the most apparent is the desire of the
government establishment to retain a hold on media which
have not, by the policies of previous administrations,
been taken over by private entrepreneurs. A second
reason could be the desire to limit the cultural and economic incursions of foreign (principally American) television signals. There is also some feeling that the

government is practising a wait-and-see policy based on
the belief that present cable techniques and practices
will soon be obsolete.

Several entrepreneurial groups want to start pay-television. Since such systems require government concessions, and since the government has shown no inclination
to grant these franchises, the plans are still shadowy.
But they should not be discounted.

It is felt that, in regard to cable systems of all
kinds and other innovative technologies of transmission
and reception, the legislature has worked to impede private enterprise. There is a great deal of pressure
within the government itself to update legislation to take
account of technical developments. The present Ley Federal de Radio y Televisión is under study and proposed modifications are being prepared for Congress. It is hoped
that these changes may give some impetus to the development of commercial video systems other than the established conventional systems now in use.

The creation of the Dirección General de Radio, Televisión y Cinematografía (RTC) seems to have engendered a
rather more optimistic attitude and this, combined with
the above-mentioned modifications in the communications
law, gives promise of important major changes in the industry.

Unlike television, radio seems to be consonant with
the socio-economic realities of the country, and the receivers now in use. Although FM stereo exists and is
popular, there is no widespread movement in the industry
to advance to AM stereo or any quadraphonic system. The
almost universal distribution of radio sets, many of them
transistorised battery receivers, is not favourable to the
introduction of new modes since the majority of listeners
could not afford the costly replacements necessary.

In spite of the steps taken by the major radio organisations towards advances in technology, the broadcasting
industry is acutely aware of changing listening habits and
needs. In fact, most radio and television executives
clearly express the viewpoint that this is a time of continuing change in mass tastes. It is imperative to
recognise the influence of young people on the mass media.
Almost 59 per cent of the Mexican population is under
twenty and 65 per cent is under twenty-five; almost two-
thirds of the total population. The effect of emerging

Chapter 6

adults is cumulative and powerful on both radio and television. Consequently both electronic media invest in continuous quantitative and qualitative research. There is a growing interest in the television field in the use of direct feedback and it appears to be quite certain that such systems will be adopted when they are proved to be technically feasible.

Superficially, the Mexican systems may appear to parallel or imitate systems in other countries. This superficial resemblance is deceptive. Mexican broadcasting was born in chaos and grew under peculiarly idiosyncratic social, economic and political pressures which have given it its essential form. Two characteristic phenomena separate Mexican broadcasting from other apparently similar operations. The first is the tradition of 'fiscal time', which gives the government access to radio and television time without forcing it to become a broadcaster. The second and probably more important factor is applicable only to television and is the co-existence of state, quasi-state and private enterprise. The different forms of ownership and management in Mexico have, until this time, been essentially constructive. The hybrid nature of Channel 13, a quasi-state enterprise, places the government in a Janus-like position. It must think and act as a private enterprise without, at the same time, losing its abilities as an administrative entity to deal with the communications industry at arms-length. The government must, therefore, make the best of both systems in order to be politically consistent and functionally effective.

Such a condition might be seen as artificial and inhibiting. In fact it has stimulated the creation of a *modus vivendi*. The philosophy that permits the functioning of disparate forms of ownership is a belief in alternative systems that are mutually tolerant and, at present, not on any collision course. The system is showing great vigour and measures up well against the yardstick of reality. In all probability this tripartite form of co-existence will continue to be the pattern for Mexican television in the foreseeable future.

Appendix 1

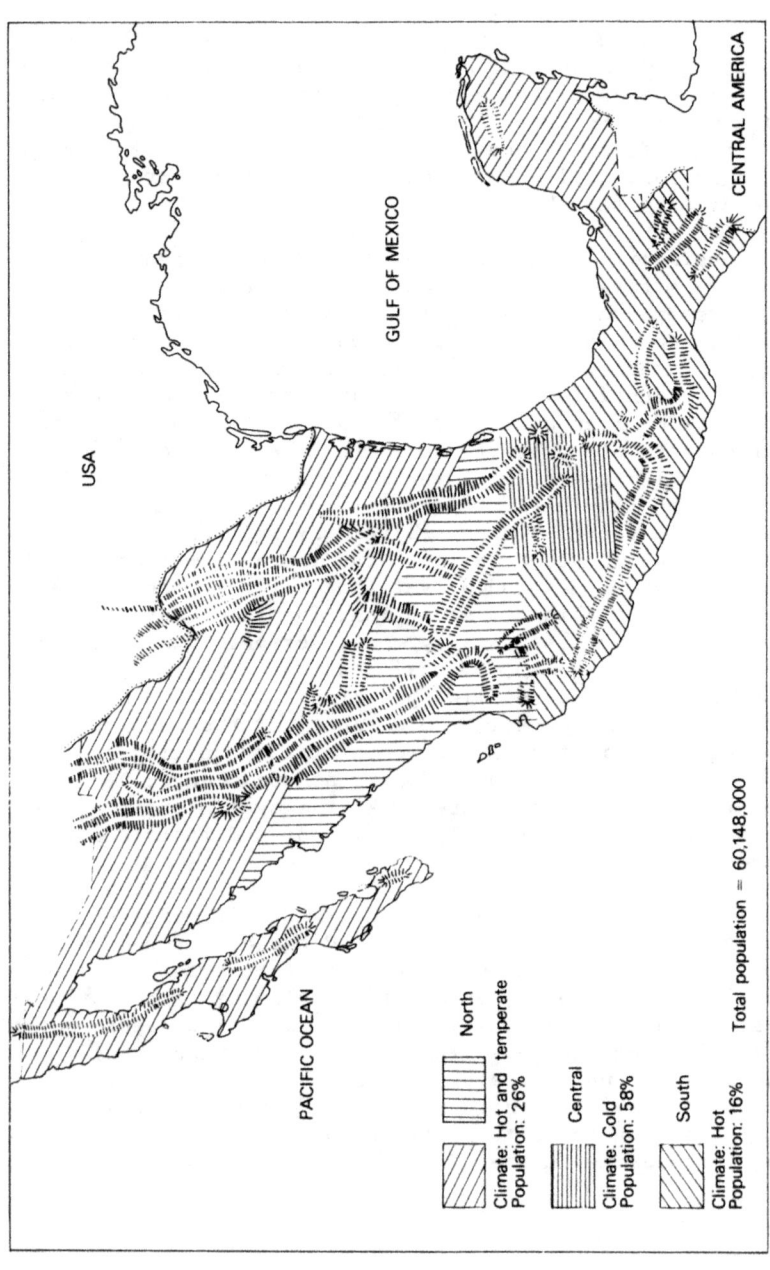

MAP OF MEXICO

Appendix 2

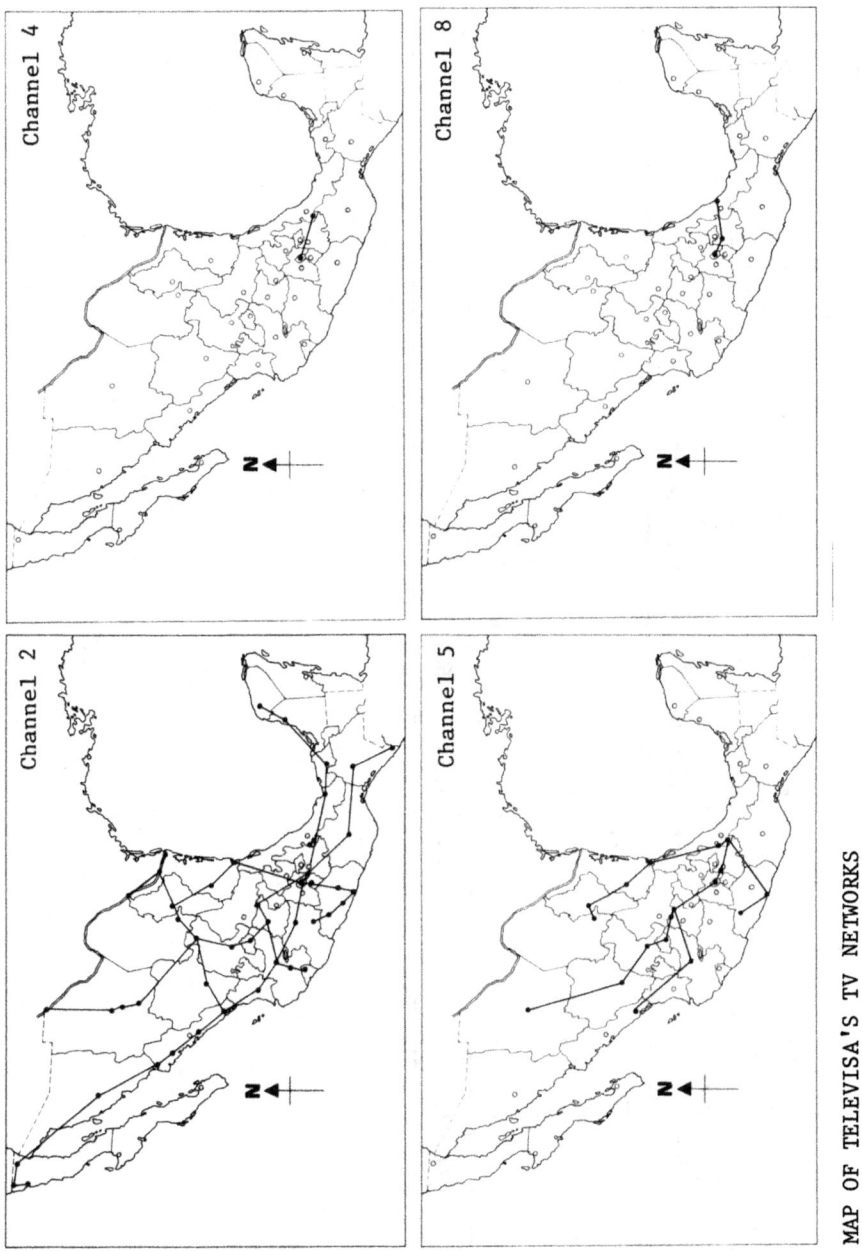

MAP OF TELEVISA'S TV NETWORKS

83

Appendix 3

Televisa: comparative analysis of broadcasting hours and local and foreign production, per year (June 1976-7)

	Transmission hours	%	Local production	%	Foreign production	%
Channel 2	6,342:16	100	5,524:07	87.1	818:09	12.9
Channel 4	3,747:28	100	3,357:44	89.6	389:44	10.4
Channel 5	6,477:28	100	3,089:45	47.7	3,387:43	52.3
Channel 8	4,855:56	100	1,068:18	22.0	3,787:38	78.0
TOTAL	21,423:08	100	13,039:54	60.9	8,383:14	39.1

Appendix 4

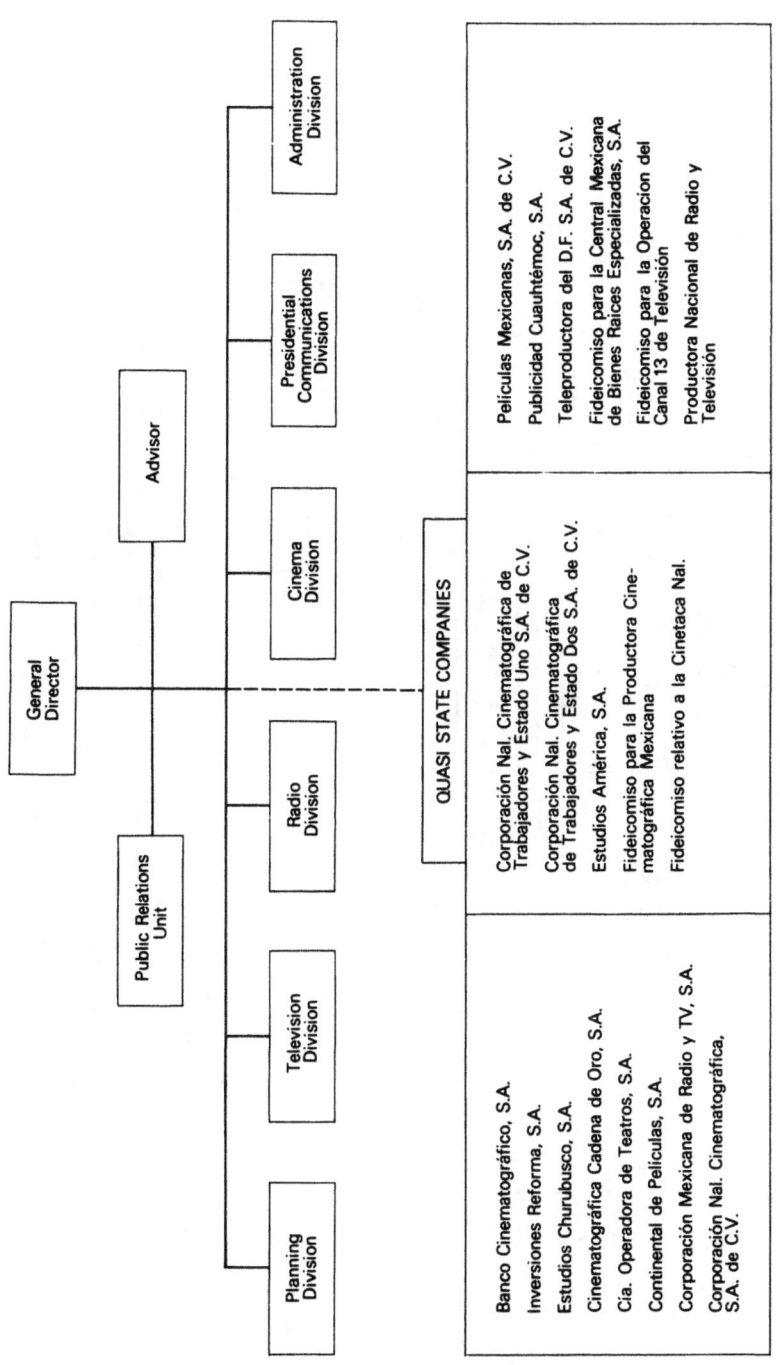

DIRECCION GENERAL DE RADIO, TELEVISION Y CINEMATOGRAFIA:
ORGANISATION CHART

Appendix 5

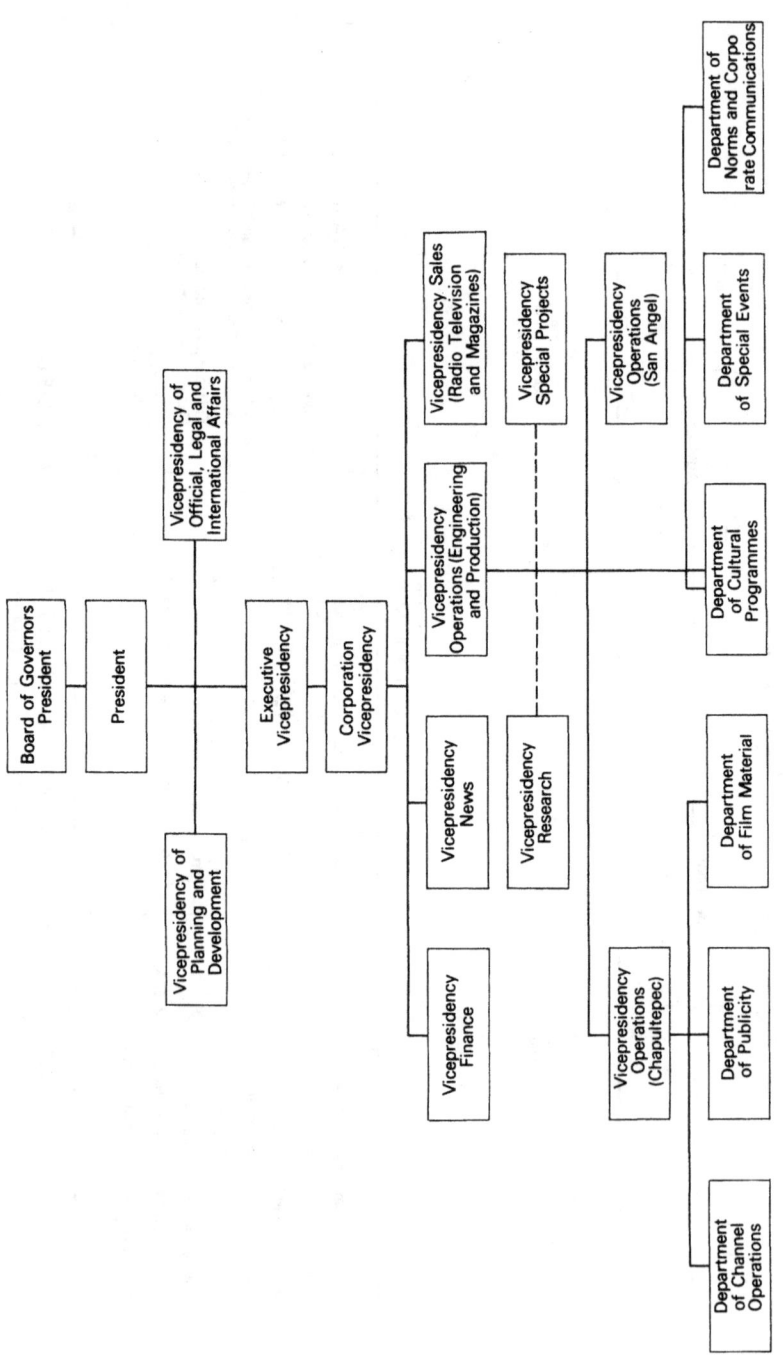

TELEVISA: ORGANISATION CHART

BIBLIOGRAPHY

I BOOKS

ALDAMA, ALFREDO, 'La Televisión en México', Ed. Progreso, Mexico, 1973.
ALVEAR ACEVEDO, CARLOS, 'Manual de Historia de la Cultura', Ed. Jus, Mexico, 1972.
COSÍO VILLEGAS, DANIEL et al., 'Historia Mínima de México', El Colegio de México, Mexico, 1974.
HANSEN, ROGER, 'Política del Desarrollo Económico de México', Ed. Siglo XXI, Mexico, 1974.
MEJÍA PRIETO, JORGE, 'Historia de la Radio y la Televisión en México', Ed. Octavio Colmenares, Mexico, 1972.
VERNON, RAYMOND, 'El Dilema del Desarrollo Económico de México', Ed. Diana, Mexico, 1973.

II MAGAZINES

ALEMÁN VELASCO, MIGUEL, El Estado y la Television, in 'Nueva Política', vol. 1, no. 3, September 1976.
'Antena', Revista Cámara Nacional de la Industria de Radio y Televisión - nos 37, 39, 42, 47, 52, 53, 56, 57, 58, 59, 62, 63, 64, Mexico, 1975, 1976, 1977.
GRANADOS CHAPA, MIGUEL A., La Televisión de Estado, in 'Nueva Política', vol. 1, no. 3, September 1976.

III DICTIONARIES AND ENCYCLOPEDIAS

'Diccionario Porrúa de Historia, Biografía y Geografía de México', Ed. Porrua, Mexico, 1976.
'Enciclopedia Universal Illustrada Europeo-Americana', Ed. Espasa-Calpe, Madrid, 1958.

IV REPORTS

'Anuario de la Cámara Nacional de la Industria de Radio y Televisión' (CIRT), 1976.
'Censo Estadístico 1970', Dirección General de Estadística, Secretaría de Industria y Comercio.
'Directorio MPM de Medios', Medios Publicitarios Mexicanos, June 1977.
'Informe Septiembre 1º, 1975 a Agosto 31, 1976', INDECO.
'Memoria de la Subsecretaría de Radiodifusión', 1970-6.
'Mexico en Cifras 1975', Banco Nacional de México, SA.
'Resumen de Actividades 1970-1976', Instituto Nacional Indigenista.
SPAIN, PETER L., 'A Report on the System of Radioprimaria in the State of San Luis Potosí, Mexico', Institute for Communication Research, Stanford University, March 1973.
'Telesecundaria', Dirección General de Educación Audiovisual Secretaria de Educación Pública (SEP), 1976.

V STUDIES AND THESIS

'Análisis Multi-Media', Comunicología Aplicada de México AC, Mexico, 1976.
DE ANDA Y RAMOS, FRANCISCO, 'La Radiodifusión en el Valle de México y su Apego a la Ley', Universidad Iberoamericana, Mexico, 1973.
DONNEAUD, GERARDO, 'Análisis de Contenido de las canciones más populares y vendidas en México, D.F. de junio de 1973 a junio de 1974, en base a su temática, la intensidad de su contenido emocional y a los valores que proyectan referentes a la Teoría del carácter de Erich Fromm', Universidad Iberoamericana, Mexico, 1975.

VI LEGAL TEXTS

Constitución Política de los Estados Unidos Mexicanos.
Ley Federal de Radio y Televisión.
Artículos de la Ley de Vías Generales de Comunicación relacionados con Radio y Televisión.
Ley de Ingresos de la Federación para el Ejercicio Fiscal de 1969. (Decreto publicado en el Diario Oficial de la Federación el 31 de diciembre de 1968.)
Presupuesto de Egresos de la Federación, que regirá durante el año de 1969. (Decreto publicado en el Diario Oficial de la Federación el 30 de diciembre de 1968.)
Acuerdo Presidencial que establece el régimen actual de concesiones (publicado en el Diario Oficial de la Federación el 1º de julio de 1969).

Decreto Presidencial que establece que el Canal 11 de
televisión se utilizará para la transmisión de programas
educativos, culturales y de orientación social. (Publicado en el Diario Oficial de la Federación el 2 de agosto
de 1969.)
Acuerdo Presidencial que establece la Red Federal de
estaciones difusoras de televisión. (Publicado en el
Diario Oficial de la Federación el 6 de agosto de 1969.)
Acuerdo Presidencial que establece la Comisión Inter-
secretarial en materia de radio y televisión. (Publicado
en el Diario Oficial de la Federación el 21 de agosto de
1969.)
Acuerdo Presidencial por el que se crea la Dirección
General de Información y Relaciones Públicas. (Publicado
en el Diario Oficial de la Federación el 1? de junio de
1977.)
Decreto Presidencial por el que se crea la Productora
Nacional de Radio y Televisión. (Publicado en el Diario
Oficial de la Federación el 4 de julio de 1977.)
Reglamento Interior de la Secretaría de Gobernación.
(Publicado en el Diario Oficial de la Federación el 6 de
julio de 1977.)

For Product Safety Concerns and Information please contact our EU
representative GPSR@taylorandfrancis.com
Taylor & Francis Verlag GmbH, Kaufingerstraße 24, 80331 München, Germany

www.ingramcontent.com/pod-product-compliance
Lightning Source LLC
Chambersburg PA
CBHW061420300426
44114CB00015B/2009